AWAKENING
THE CHURCH
IN NORTH AMERICA

AWAKENING THE CHURCH IN NORTH AMERICA

J. DAVID STEPHENS
FOREWORD BY TIMOTHY M. HILL

Pathway

Scripture quotations marked GW are taken from God's Word, which is a copyrighted work of God's Word to the Nations Bible Society. Quotations are used by permission. Copyright © 1995 by God's Word to the Nations Bible Society. All rights reserved.

Scripture quotations marked KJV are taken from the King James Version of the Bible.

Scripture quotations marked NIV are taken from The Holy Bible, New International Version®. NIV®. Copyright © 1973, 1978, 1984, 2011 by International Bible Society. Used by permission of Zondervan Publishing House. All rights reserved.

Scripture quotations marked NKJV are taken from the New King James Version. Copyright © 1979, 1980, 1982, 1990, 1995, Thomas Nelson, Inc., Publishers.

Scripture quotations marked NRSV are taken from the New Revised Standard Version of the Bible. Copyright © 1989 by the Division of Christian Education of the National Council of the Churches of Christ in the USA. Used by permission.

Scripture quotations marked Ph. (or Phillips) are taken from The New Testament in Modern English Revised Edition. Copyright © 1958, 1959, 1960, 1972 by J. B. Phillips. Reprinted with permission of Macmillan Publishing Company.

Scripture quotations marked TLB are taken from The Living Bible. Copyright © 1971. Used by permission of Tyndale House Publishers, Inc., Wheaton, IL 60189. All rights reserved.

ISBN: 978-1-64288-049-6

Copyright © 2019 by Pathway Press
Cleveland, Tennessee 37311

All rights reserved. No part of this publication may be reproduced or transmitted in any form or by any means, electronic or mechanical, including photocopying, recording, or otherwise, or by any information storage or retrieval system, without the permission in writing from the publisher. Please direct inquiries to Pathway Press, 1080 Montgomery Avenue, Cleveland, TN 37311.

Visit www.pathwaypress.org for more information.

Printed in the United States of America

CONTENTS

FOREWORD 9

PREFACE 11

ACKNOWLEDGEMENTS 21

INTRODUCTION 23

1 "RISE UP, O CHURCH OF GOD". 33

2 SPIRITUAL DNA MATTERS 57

3 REVIVING WHAT REMAINS 77

4 PROACTIVE IN POST-CHRISTIAN
  CULTURE 101

5 COMMUNICATION THAT CONNECTS .. 115

6 CONSIDERING YESTERDAY
  CONCEIVING TOMORROW 141

7 REACHING WHEREVER YOU ARE 159

8 AWAKEN TO YOUR PURPOSE! 195

  ENDORSEMENTS 203

Author's Notes

1. *In the Division of Evangelization for the Church of God, Mission North America is referenced in terms of serving the United States and Canada. This terminology works well when it is understood that Mexico and other countries on the North American continent are served by World Missions.*

2. *When the word church is used throughout this book, please notice that it is sometimes capitalized (Church). This is when referring to the larger body of Christ (worldwide or North American). Otherwise, it will be lowercase in all other circumstances—such as the local church or a specific denomination.*

FOREWORD

Anyone born in the 1960s, or before the so-called "Baby Boomers," can recall the days when the USA and Canada were viewed as countries where missionaries were sent out to "save the world." Both countries were referred to as overwhelmingly Christian, and natives of these countries took pride (rightfully or not) in proclaiming that evangelism was needed more "beyond our borders," than within them.

Over the last few decades that scenario has shifted. While the USA and Canada still send missionaries, other countries have overtaken them. Latin American countries outshine their northern counterparts in evangelistic fervor, while African nations regularly attract hundreds of thousands to Christian crusades.

So, what is the answer for the USA and Canada to recapture the Pentecostal fire that once burned afresh as it did in the early 1900s? How do we empower the current and future generations to bring back the "glory days" of a hunger for the move of God?

J. David Stephens is uniquely qualified to recognize not only where we have been, but also how we might return to those days of being on the front lines of evangelism. Born into a minister's home and subsequently called into ministry at an early age, he has lived in Canada and in virtually every region of the United States where he was either a pastor, state youth director, or state overseer. Jim Stephens has also spent the last seven years on the International Executive Committee of the Church of God, further enhancing his authority on solutions toward reviving the effectiveness of the USA and Canada in reaching the harvest.

Awakening the Church in North America will inspire those who may feel these two countries have lost their ability to bring themselves back to God. Indeed, it offers tools and resources for that journey and offers a path for us all as we strive toward FINISHing the Great Commission.

Tim Hill
General Overseer
CHURCH OF GOD
Cleveland, Tennessee

PREFACE

Recognize—Recalibrate—Replenish

Born in Hamilton, Ohio, I was the only boy among four children of James and Edna Stephens. My dad was a Church of God pastor. Every church he pastored grew and loved him, my mother, and our family. It was a great life. We didn't have a life of luxury by any means, but we were a happy family that loved the Church. Dad also was a state overseer during my childhood and teen years. We lived in various regions of North America, from Western Canada to Florida, before I finished college.

My experience growing up in the Church of God gave me a unique perspective. My earliest recollection of life began in the western plains of Saskatchewan, Canada, where my father served as overseer and president of International Bible College. We lived on the small rural campus near Estevan and were part of the school family. It seemed as if we were farmers of a sort.

AWAKENING THE CHURCH IN NORTH AMERICA

From childhood, until I left home to attend Lee University, my father served as state overseer of Indiana, Pennsylvania, Virginia, and Florida. Understandably, my experience in the church was fairly different from my wife's where she grew up in a lay couple's home and they were faithful members of a local church. Unlike Joyce, I understood the church from a broader perspective, much like a large, extended family with local, district, state, regional, and international expressions.

My wife, Joyce, has a different view and perspective of what the church is to her. Since birth, the church was and remains a major part of her life. As devout and faithful Christians, her non-ministerial parents saw the value of the church and raised her to love everything about it. From toddler to high school years, Joyce's family faithfully attended just two churches—one in Toledo, Ohio, and the other after they moved, in Monroe, Michigan.

Their family never missed a service, whether Sunday mornings, evenings, Wednesday night, revivals, district and camp meetings, youth camp, and so on. Even though both parents worked full-time jobs, and were tired and worn out, they never missed church and they never *made* Joyce go to church; she wanted to be there!

PREFACE

Though both of the two churches Joyce's family attended were different, they both had the same key characteristics. Church members in the Toledo, Segur Avenue Church of God, truly loved the Lord, loved each other, and especially loved the children. Church was a happy and joyful place for Joyce.

Joyce recalls feeling uncomfortable one Sunday when a motorcycle gang came into the church. They sat on the back two rows, laughing and carrying on in a disruptive way. The Holy Spirit started moving and some of those young men started weeping. Several went to the altar that night and gave their hearts to the Lord. The gang continued to come to church, but they were never disruptive again. Church members began to show great love and concern for them. Joyce knew the Holy Spirit must be real when she witnessed all these things.

When Joyce was about seven years old, she got the measles and it somehow affected her ears. Apparently, it was serious because the family pediatrician came to their house. Her parents were told her eardrums might burst, so they stayed up all night with her for several nights. Joyce clearly recalls two elderly sisters from the church coming to her house and praying the entire night by her bedside. The next morning, Joyce was better and her ears were healed! In situations like these and others, my wife "caught" who God is instead of just being "taught" who He is. By living for Christ exactly the same way, both outside and inside the church, Joyce's church family made a huge impression on her, and she wanted to be just like them.

In Monroe, Joyce and her family attended a larger church with about 400 attending. All the workers in the church were volunteers who worked full-time jobs, but they felt called to work for the church too. The people in this church were also loving, kind, supportive, and they genuinely loved their young people. There were always lots of hugs, love, and words of affirmation to the young people from the adults of the church. Joyce remembers feeling she just always wanted to be around them.

As a teenager, Joyce learned lessons that lasted a lifetime.

- God's Word shows us how to live.
- The Holy Spirit gives us boldness, guides us, and directs us to invite others to serve the Lord.
- Prayer is a personal relationship with Jesus. We can take everything to Him, knowing He listens and cares.

PREFACE

- It is okay to have questions!
- The youth and children were taught to love the church and to love church leaders. They were heroes in the eyes of the youth! Joyce indicates she never lost respect and honor for the church's leaders. The pastor encouraged and explained church membership. Joyce joined the church at sixteen years old. She believed the church's teachings would provide a more meaningful life and keep her from harm.
- Joyce learned that being a leader in the church was a choice not to be taken lightly.
- Your walk needs to match your talk.
- Our parents and adults in the church are for us, and we can trust and cherish each other. The adults attended many of Joyce's high school events, her graduation, and her wedding; she felt loved!
- Teenagers can make a difference for the Lord. The high school knew about her church because the teens won many to the Lord. People in the community were eager to hire kids from that church for jobs.
- Tithing was for her good, and it would bless the church and others. Joyce recalls feeling a spirit of

AWAKENING THE CHURCH IN NORTH AMERICA

awe when she filled out a tithe envelope or fulfilled a World Missions pledge.

- Life is not easy. Sometimes hard, difficult, and sad times come to everyone. Joyce observed her family and other families in the church go through many rough times, but she also noted they did not give up—the Lord gave them the strength they needed.

- Joyce's local church was a "sending church." Church of God churches around North America today are pastored by people who were raised at the Stewart Road church in Monroe, Michigan.

Even now, being in full-time ministry with me for all these years, Joyce's desire to be an instrument in building the local church remains, because her local church did so much to build her.

During my late teens and early twenties, before I met Joyce, I decided to put my formal education on the backburner to evangelize for about two years. I went wherever pastors, predominantly in Virginia, invited me. Those were good years that allowed for observing churches from a neutral and impartial perspective. I learned a great deal, including how to preach and communicate in many different congregational styles and sizes.

PREFACE

After graduating from Lee University in 1972, Joyce and I married and planted the Church of God in Stafford, Virginia, launching a ministry journey that eventually took us to the West, Northwest, Midwest, Southeast, and Northeast, in that order, principally serving wherever the church asked and the Holy Spirit led. We had a very positive church-planting experience because the Lord blessed us with some great people. After renting a small house for about eight months, we purchased eight acres of land. By the end of our second year, we had built a church building. After pastoring in Stafford four years and with more than two hundred people attending each Sunday, we moved cross-country to Arizona as the state youth and Christian education director, initiating us into longstanding service in church administration and leadership.

As the second assistant general overseer since 2012, and simultaneously fulfilling the roles of executive director of the Division of Education for four years, with four additional years as executive director of the Division of World Evangelization, I have a rather vast and rich understanding about this movement. For example, I have close relationship with national and regional leaders, pastors, and ministers of Canada as that nation's Executive Committee liaison. My personal variety of ministry experiences is certainly not the norm for most, because it provided me an immensely broad, multidimensional, multifaceted purview, knowledge, and understanding of the Church of God in North America, which I so deeply love.

For more than forty years now, I have considered myself as an assistant pastor of sorts to thousands of churches. As odd as that may sound, it is precisely how I approached being the state youth director of seven states, and state overseer of four. Sometimes that meant helping individual churches, youth leaders, and pastors. My ambition was to resource them, collectively and individually, by delivering preeminent training opportunities and experiences. My goal was (and still is) to strengthen, nurture, and inspire churches, pastors, and leaders by designing life-giving processes and experiences, and to deliver all of those with excellence and anointing.

My conviction remains that the regional, state, and International Offices exist for the fundamental purpose of serving and resourcing the local church. I have done my very best to make the local church my first priority!

PREFACE

Engaging hundreds of local churches toward forward-thinking ministry is my lifetime priority. I also continue to be intentional about forging and maintaining one-on-one relationships with as many pastors and church leaders as possible. Out of unending, abounding love for this church, its history, people, and future, I humbly offer this book with the hope of seeing a genuine, unmistakable, Spirit-led renewal, replenishment, and revitalization of the Church in North America.

ACKNOWLEDGEMENTS

Randall Parris' energy for this project has been amazing. He has been my personal coach and the book project manager. His skill in organizing and facilitating all the moving parts, as well as his persistence in staying on course, have been priceless!

Veva Rose has served as my executive assistant during the last several years and has been a key player from the concept to the finished product of the book. Her expertise and eye for excellence is embedded throughout this project.

Tammy Milner has been my resident proofreader and copy editor from the early drafts to the finished product. She has been a most valuable team member.

I am indebted to the dozens of admired colleagues who shared their experience and insights on ministry. Without their conversations, encouragements, and personal stories, I would not have been able to do this project.

AWAKENING THE CHURCH IN NORTH AMERICA

I am especially grateful to the seven dynamic people who took on the gigantic task of being collaborative coaches. They have been significant in the development of the various topics that help define this book's purpose. Every team member is listed in the foreword, and also at the conclusion of the section on which they collaborated.

INTRODUCTION

*Pair the Bluetooth and charge the remote; connect the
selfie stick, keep it steady, and take the photo!*

Pairing technical devices by utilizing something
called *Bluetooth* at one time may sound like outer-space
talk, but it is everyday conversation now. Similar to
global positioning systems (GPS), *Bluetooth* is a wireless,
inexpensive, automatic conduit for disseminating
information in real time. Its use is indicative of today's
modern communication highway. Therefore, ministers
and churches must understand how a wireless, Bluetooth-
connected, selfie-photo culture engages the world.

However, this book is not about new technology.
Awakening the Church in North America is about a red-
hot passion for the Holy Spirit to restore power to
languishing ministries, and for ministers to recapture the
quintessential zeal, the *Like a Mighty Army* confidence that
energized the church in our first one hundred years.

This book shares the analyses from a long-running collaborative conversation concerning the urgent need for resurgence of the Evangelical Church in Canada and United States. This work is composed by like-minded people who have lived in the Church of God, a Pentecostal Movement most of their lives. Some were born in the church; others grew up with parents, grandparents, and iconic church leaders. Some came later in life—all ages, genders, and ministry experiences. This collaborative effort represents the pulsebeat of many friends and colleagues in ministry.

There has been a persuasive initiative led by Project Pray founder, P. Douglas Small, for robust prayer focusing on intimacy with the Holy Spirit and seeking His direction for the Church.

In 2011, Dr. Raymond F. Culpepper, former general overseer, edited a comprehensive book: *The Great Commission*. It is an evangelism encyclopedia that fleshes out a vision and pathway for the Church of God to fulfill the Great Commission of Matthew 28:19-20.

In 2013, another influential leader and former general overseer, Dr. Mark L. Williams, coauthored with Dr. Lee Roy Martin, *Spirit-Filled Preaching in the 21st Century*. In

INTRODUCTION

it, they lift up the Church's dependence on Holy Spirit anointing for effectively preaching the Gospel.

This volume is informed and inspired by General Overseer Timothy Hill's challenge to FINISH the Great Commission with overwhelming victory in this new millennium. I pray it will resonate with you and stir up the gift that God has placed within you.

Awakening the Church in North America is a collective project—each contributor loves the doctrine and mission of the Church of God and is committed to our future. This book is not an attempt to address every issue facing evangelicals and pentecostals. It is not a survey of 10,000 people, a "Barna-style" report, or an attempt to exhaustively address every current pressing subject Bible teaching churches are encountering. However, it presents honest insight and foresight to reap today's harvest for the Church of our Lord, Jesus Christ.

Awakening the Church in North America

Book Contributors:

Michael Alley	Marty Baker	Michael Ball
Harold Bare	Teddie Bennett	Eliezer Bonilla
J. J. Chiara	James Cossey	Bryan Cutshall
Jason Daughdrill	Bruce Deel	Richard Dial
Chris Gilbert	David Gosnell	Chad Guyton
Larry Hasmatali	Les Higgins	Kyle Hinson
Jason Isaacs	James Izzard Jr.	Travis Johnson
Michael Knight	William Lee Jr.	Gary Lewis
Amy McGlamery	Rob Maggard	Mitchell Maloney
Lee Roy Martin	Jamie Massey	Tobey Montgomery
Tim Moslander	Michael Nations	R. C. Hugh Nelson
Sean O'Neal	B. Randall Parris	D. J. Portell
Mark Proctor	Michael Reynolds	B. Doyle Roberts
David Roebuck	Samuel Santana	David Smith
Jacqueline Smith	Brent Stephens	Joyce S. Stephens
Tony Stewart	Larry Timmerman	Mitchell Tolle
Dan Tomberlin	Lennox Walker	Clifton West
Rick Whitter	Mark L. Williams	

Our thesis is simple. First, the last-century Church in North America was pioneering, entrepreneurial, courageous, and ever-expanding. It was a church obsessed with evangelism—sending missionaries everywhere—across town, the region, the states, and all over the world. Our beginning, though met with opposition, was strong and the church grew rapidly.

INTRODUCTION

Second, the majority of the Church in Canada and the United States is experiencing decline. Historical data from George Barna shows that rates of church attendance, religious affiliation, belief in God, prayer, and Bible-reading have consistently dropped for decades in North America. In 1900, 80 percent of the Christians in the world lived in Europe and America. But in 2000, 60 percent of the Christians in the world were found in Asia, Africa, and Latin America. Things have changed! While we can be thankful for so many tremendous and successful ministries in North America, the reality remains that most churches are plateaued, if not in regression. Sadly, most churches in North America are realizing stagnation with few spiritual results. Even many legacy churches are struggling—few report new converts, and new members are often simply transferring from other churches.

There are obvious and understandable reasons for decline in some situations. Certainly, the goal here is not to point fingers and assign blame. Causing leaders and members to feel inadequate is never a solution for a good path forward. Hopefully, this discussion will stir God-called men and women to their place of ministry, and

AWAKENING THE CHURCH IN NORTH AMERICA

to be part of the awakening so desperately needed in the Church in North America.

As this church continues well into the second hundred years of ministry, may the Holy Spirit bring renewal to discover afresh the spiritual DNA that once moved the church forward, indeed, as a mighty army.

What were the strengths of our forefathers and foremothers? What was in their hearts? What did they value most? What did they see in God's Word and uncover in prayer that encouraged and sustained them? What were the topics of their gatherings and ministers meetings? Can we identify and repurpose the driving principles that created the zeal of those first one hundred years?

What about the success stories of today? What is in the hearts of men and women who are reaching the unchurched, making disciples, and growing the Kingdom? What can be learned from them?

People are the sole reason Christ came to earth—to live and minister; to be crucified and rise from the dead. He did all of this to redeem and reconcile the world. He gave the Church the keys to the Kingdom to continue His mission of seeking and saving the lost. People need the Lord, and He reaches them through the ministry of His Church.

INTRODUCTION

Rise up, O church of God!
Have done with lesser things;
Give heart and mind and soul and strength
To serve the King of kings.

Rise up, O children of God!
The church for you doth wait,
Her strength unequal to her task;
Rise up and make her great.

Lift high the cross of Christ;
Tread where His feet have trod;
As foll'wers of the Son of Man,
Rise up, O church of God.

(Fetke, Tom; Williams, Aaron; Merrill, William. "Rise Up, O Church of God!", Integrity Pd Arrangement, Copyright © 1997. All rights reserved. Used by permission.)

I challenge you to initiate conversations with your friends and fellow ministers about the spiritual DNA that birthed this movement, and how each one must do what is necessary to advance Christ's Church today. God is calling the church in North America and around the world to dream new dreams and see new visions.

J. David Stephens,
Assistant General Overseer
CHURCH OF GOD
Cleveland, Tennessee

DEDICATION

I dedicate this book to Joyce, my sweetheart, wife, and ministry teammate for the last forty years. Joyce is, bar-none, the most influential and esteemed person in my life. Thank you, Joyce.

I dedicate this book to our son and daughter, their spouses, and all our grandchildren. We love them dearly and are very proud of the passion they have for Christ and His Church! Brent and his wife, Sarah, pastor in Acworth, Georgia, with their four children, James David, Abbey, Bryar, and Hannah. Our daughter, Jeanna, and her husband, J. J. Chiara, pastor in Easton, Pennsylvania, with their three children, Ava, Mary, and Harrison. Thank you, children and grandchildren, for being mentors to me, and for the joy you bring into my life.

I dedicate this book to my parents, James and Edna Stephens. There is no greater father or mother . . . and no greater ministers of the Gospel. They were godly examples who loved Jesus and His Church more than their lives. Faithful ministers in the Church of God, they served with a sense of calling to this denomination. Thank you, Mom and Dad.

I dedicate this book to the ministers, pastors, leaders, and church members who are dearer to me than words can express. Our times together continue to be a source of strength to me. You are the best—thank you.

1

"RISE UP, O CHURCH OF GOD"

"I will build My church, and the gates of Hades shall not prevail against it" (Matthew 16:18 NKJV).

A few years ago, I sat in a large and successful Christian school auditorium. One of my granddaughters was in the school Christmas program. We arrived early, so people were still coming in. Three couples moved in behind me, Joyce, and my son's family. Overhearing their conversation as they settled into their seats simply could not be avoided. It was obvious by their discussion that one of the couples was church-shopping. One of the young women asked a captivating question: "How is your church search going? Are you finding something that you feel will work for you?"

Another woman replied, "Wow . . . it's not going very good at all. I sat down in a church recently, picked up something they had printed, and started reading about all they offer. I read about what I could be a part of; how to connect; how to participate; and I thought to myself, *I don't need this at all!"*

A man's voice chimed in immediately. "Yeah, the Church just doesn't get it! It's just not the great people-attraction it once was, and it doesn't really relate to people like it used to. Church is becoming more and more irrelevant to what people need and want. Really, church is just one of many options for Sundays." The man behind me continued, "Most people pick up the newspaper or go online on Sundays, then discuss what they want to do for the day. They may see a movie, go to the park or mall, or maybe go to church."

Honestly, hearing their conversation was not a terrible shock. Today's church is greatly undervalued by many people. It is viewed by many as more of an enrichment opportunity, not something to invest in personally or take very seriously.

Today's casual attitude toward the church, reflected in this conversation, stands in stark contrast to my appreciation for it growing up in the James and Edna Stephens family. My early childhood experience was that church was the most significant place in the world, second only to home. We engaged church at least three times a

"RISE UP, O CHURCH OF GOD"

week. The people there were our spiritual brothers and sisters, aunts and uncles. We celebrated our faith in Jesus and fought the devil together as one, big, happy family.

It is time to reclaim the church and its importance in the kingdom of God. One of the first places to look to better understand the Church is in the longest recorded prayer of Jesus found in the entire chapter of John 17. This chapter chronicles the passionate prayer of Jesus for the Church. His prayer shows His heart for the Church and the strength of the Church.

Is the Church Important? Just Ask Jesus!

The Church is God's primary instrument to fulfill His plan to redeem mankind. Christ's prayer in John 17:9 says, "I pray for them: I pray not for the world" (KJV). Think about that—I pray not for the world! Not for the lost! Not for sinners! He said: "[I pray] for them which thou hast given me." In verse 20, Jesus said, "I do not pray for these alone, but also for those who will believe in Me through their word" (NKJV). He was praying for the *Ekklesia*, the "called-out ones"—a word used 114 times in the New Testament.

There is nothing on earth more important to Jesus Christ than His Church. He is Head of the Church and

35

AWAKENING THE CHURCH IN NORTH AMERICA

all the resources of heaven are committed to the Church. This truth is understood by Christ-followers and is why they say "yes" to the many sacrifices required to serve the Church. Dr. Dan Tomberlin, an outstanding student of the Word and instructor in pastoral ministries at the Pentecostal Theological Seminary, says: "To participate in the Church is essential to be a faithful Christian. To walk away from the Church is to walk away from Christ."

> **There is nothing on earth more important to Jesus Christ than His Church. He is Head of the Church and all the resources of heaven are committed to the Church.**

Contrary to what some people think, the Church is not a man-created institution but, rather, a God-created institution. According to Jesus' remarks to Peter and all the disciples in Matthew 16, our profession of faith in Christ is essential for building His Church. He declared in verse 18: "I will build My church, and the gates of Hades shall not prevail against it" (NKJV). He loves His Church, as Paul emphatically states in Ephesians 5:25: "Christ . . . loved the church and gave himself for her." Acts 20:28 is a very powerful charge to everyone who answers the

"Rise Up, O Church of God"

call to leadership in the church: "Take heed therefore unto yourselves, and to all the flock, over the which the Holy Ghost hath made you overseers, to feed the church of God, which he hath purchased with his own blood" (KJV). The first three chapters of Ephesians gives clarity on the design, purpose, and plan of God for His Church. God's plan is to redeem His creation. He predestined the church to be His people. Jesus has all power in heaven and in earth and is the Head of the Church. All who accept the truth and believe in Christ are born into the Church; and God is glorified by the Church on earth.

Parachurch and nonprofit groups accomplish very important and needed ministry. I appreciate and support many of them financially. These are ministries and do not claim to be substitutes for the Church. However, Jesus equipped the Church like no other institution to make disciples in this world. It is very easy to muddy the waters between God's calling to ministry for everyone and God's calling to the Church. Every Christian has the responsibility to bear witness of Christ. Dr. Mark Proctor, professor of New Testament at Lee University, advocates that Christian ministry is a universal calling, but is not the same calling as taking on responsibility in the church.

Is Your Church, *the* Church?

Some wonder if the church they attend is the true body of Christ or little more than a small, closed, social group. This is a legitimate concern. The potential for a church to deviate and digress into a club or social group is an existing possibility. It takes more than a church sign, preacher, and singing a few hymns to be a church. The members of the body of Christ are the people God has called to represent Him in the world—to be visible proof of His invisible body on earth. Healthy churches are Christ's ambassadors, reconciling people in their community to God. When Jesus gave the keys to the kingdom of heaven to His Church, He was giving them a divine connection, mission, and spiritual authority— eternally, universally, and locally.

Your church may be a sleeping giant which you are finding it difficult to awaken. Just remember the two questions Jesus asked the disciples in Matthew 16. These are important questions for the church you attend. They probe the spiritual climate within the community and within the church: First, do you know what your community believes about Jesus? Second, have you "looked on the fields" and identified the harvest? Once

"RISE UP, O CHURCH OF GOD"

the ministry needs of a community are understood, the next step is to examine your faith to see if it is bold and zealous enough to spread the gospel of the Kingdom throughout your community. Pastor Chris Hodges of The Church of the Highlands in Birmingham, Alabama, clarifies four ministries for church leaders to prioritize.

1. Win the lost.

2. Pastor them.

3. Disciple them.

4. Mobilize them.

These are the real priorities of every healthy church.

What Is the Church Supposed to Do?

John 6 provides many interesting details of Jesus feeding the multitude with a young boy's lunch. This extraordinary event enabled those around Jesus to "connect the dots" of His claim to be the Son of God. The entire chapter is an eye-opening discourse. Among many heart-pounding truths discovered in this chapter, verses 28-29 appear to leap off the page. A question is asked by some of the Jews: "What shall we do, that we might work the works of God?" (v. 28 KJV). What follows is a riveting response by Jesus when He said, "This is the work of God, that ye

AWAKENING THE CHURCH IN NORTH AMERICA

believe on him whom he hath sent" (v. 29 KJV). What a transformational revelation for the Church!

In light of the current climate of systematic and intentional deconstruction of Christian faith and values in the United States, and the growing acceptance of religious pluralism, the question becomes: "What shall we do, that we might work the works of God?" Today's culture is convinced there is no absolute or universal truth and that every truth is relative. Therefore, the Church—every believer in the body of Christ—is compelled to know and embrace the work God calls us to do!

In the context of John 6, after just watching Jesus miraculously feed thousands of people, utilizing only five loaves of bread and two small fish, these Jews were asking a double-barreled question. They were asking first about God's requirements for eternal life, and second, about how to do His work on earth. In their minds, work was required to receive bread and meat, so work must also be required to attain the bread and meat that brings everlasting life. The answer Jesus gave was, "This is the work of God, that ye *believe* on Him whom He hath sent." Believing is the answer to both questions. To believe is not an abstract mental exercise. Faith in Christ is much

"RISE UP, O CHURCH OF GOD"

more than a theory or hypothesis. The apostle James clarified the connection of God's work and faith in James 2:18 of his letter when he declared: "Show me your faith without your works, and I will show you my faith by my works" (NKJV).

In John chapter 6, it is apparent that these people struggled with believing what Jesus said. Like believers today, they knew Jesus was from Nazareth, and was the son of Mary and Joseph. How could they believe Jesus was the "Bread of Life" sent down from heaven? Jesus claimed that the Bread, His own flesh, He gave was far superior to the bread that Moses gave. This concept was simply unthinkable in the minds of Jesus' contemporaries. Jesus offered Scriptural and prophetic evidence that He was the Son of God—even to the point of telling them that before their father Abraham was ever born, "I AM" (John 8:58 NKJV). Jesus knew all of them found this statement "over-the-top," so He asked, "Does this offend you?" (6:61 NKJV).

In this situation, humankind's faith struggle is quite evident. Think about the faith required and notice that verse 66 records: "From that time many of His disciples went back and walked with Him no more" (NKJV).

41

They experienced a crisis of faith, so much so that Jesus asked the Twelve, "Do you also want to go away?" (v. 67 NKJV). Ultimately, it is up to individuals to decide for themselves, *"Do I believe Jesus is who He says He is?"*

When Mary Poppins Is a Religious Experience

A few years ago, I was sitting with Joyce at a Broadway performance of *Mary Poppins*. It was virtually impossible not to notice the person sitting directly in front of us. This man was *really* into the performance! He seemed to be living in the moment. Even his body language spoke clearly of just how involved in this production he actually was. He was mesmerized and fully captivated, shaking his head in full agreement. He was engrossed—he wasn't merely *watching* a play. He was totally immersed in the moment. And then, it was as if a light turned on in my head. I realized this person was almost experiencing some type of "spiritual encounter." For him, this Broadway production was where and how his spirituality was engaged. He was not looking for anything more than a theater musical to feed his spiritual man. For him, this was the primary expression of his spiritual interface. His spiritual thirst was quenched by the splendor, grace, and beauty of the Broadway production of *Mary Poppins*.

"RISE UP, O CHURCH OF GOD"

Only *living water* found through Jesus Christ can quench that thirst.

General and Specific Revelation

Walking on the beach for any length of time and watching the ocean often produces a sense of wonder and awe. The power and beauty of this experience can lead toward the possible conclusion that the ocean is the work of a Master Designer. The ocean can spark the thought that somewhere in the universe, there is a Supreme Master Planner and Sustainer. The magnificent ocean is just that amazing.

Likewise, a gorgeous panoramic mountain view can cause that same sense of astonishment and reverence. These are real-life experiences, and like the experience of the man at the Broadway musical, it may, to some degree, open someone to a spiritual experience. Nature can draw people toward belief in God. Nature, creation, and other amazing things of beauty in the universe broadcast and pronounce that there must surely be a God. A person may conclude, intuitively, that there is a God. But this is not the case with identifying and acknowledging Jesus. The gospel of Jesus Christ is not intuitive—*someone must tell of His birth, life, death, and resurrection.* As promised in the Old Testament and revealed in the New, Jesus is our Kinsman-Redeemer. This is the *Gospel* (the "good news")—the power of God that brings salvation to all who believe!

Believing Is No Small Thing

Like those first disciples, many today struggle with the claims of Christ. The truth is, God is asking humankind to believe in something that is difficult to fully comprehend. Many hear the message but are not able to receive it. They say, "It is too hard, who can understand it?" (see John 6:60). Some follow Him to a point, but then walk away. Perhaps most people want to fully believe, but there are times when people find themselves feeling like the father in Mark 9, who went to the disciples asking for help for his sick son. When they could not heal the boy, he cried out, "Lord, I believe; help my unbelief!" (v. 24 NKJV).

For some, the very scripture that serves as the typical definition of faith is also hard to fully grasp: "Now faith is the substance of things hoped for, the evidence of things not seen" (Heb. 11:1 NKJV). Does this mean we should have faith for everything we want? Does this mean we should claim things we don't have? Is something wrong with our faith if we don't get what we hope for?

"Rise Up, O Church of God"

With so many voices claiming the same faith roots in our tribe, some may find themselves asking, "What If I don't believe exactly as everyone else in the church? Am I supposed to believe everything that other Christians believe, and exactly in the same way they believe it?" The Church must allow room for minor differences and variances on some issues of faith. Having different views should not divide the church! Just like Democrats and Republicans are all Americans, as long as God's Word is the standard, room must be made for various expressions of faith.

Jesus said: "Believe," but He did not say to necessarily believe what all our friends believe. He did not say to believe for whatever our hearts desire. He did not even say to believe exactly what those we love and respect believe. Jesus was very specific when He said, "Believe on him whom he hath sent" (John 6:29 KJV). The greatest hindrance to the Church is typically not from the outside, but the inside. There is a growing number in the Church who are not sure who Jesus is. Can Christ-followers truly expect to convince the unsaved if they don't fully believe Jesus is Emmanuel—"God with us?" If Christians are not totally convinced, how will they represent Him with authority, or be empowered to do the work He commissioned the Church to do?

The Church's Power Comes by Believing

Unwavering faith in Jesus Christ is the message! To believe Him and His Word is a Christian's primary work and ministry. Life-giving ministry is the fruit of active faith. Ministry is the natural product of people who truly believe and live out their faith. God works as His disciples work out their salvation and walk in obedient faith. Additional church programs and opportunities are helpful, but these are not the strength or power of the Church's mission.

The Church must be sensitive to unbelievers and those who are in the "valley of decision." However, the Church must also be unwavering with a firm commitment to the person of Jesus Christ, just as the apostle John states in 2 John 7-11:

> Many deceivers, who do not acknowledge Jesus Christ as coming in the flesh, have gone out into the world. Any such person is the deceiver and the antichrist. Watch out that you do not lose what we have worked for, but that you may be rewarded fully. Anyone who runs ahead and does not continue in the teaching of Christ does not have God; whoever continues in the

"RISE UP, O CHURCH OF GOD"

teaching has both the Father and the Son. If anyone comes to you and does not bring this teaching, do not take them into your house or welcome them. Anyone who welcomes them shares in their wicked work (NIV).

Unlike many who try to suggest otherwise, Jesus is not "one path among many" to God. Faith in Jesus Christ is the only path to salvation and the only way to the heavenly Father. The Book of Acts proclaims, "Neither is there salvation in any other: for there is none other name under heaven given among men, whereby we must be saved" (4:12 KJV).

It cannot be overstated. Believe! Believe! Believe! This is the mandate of the Church. The primary work of God emanates as His children fully believe in Him. The message and mission begin and end in Him. Jesus is still the answer. He is "the same yesterday, today, and forever" (Heb. 13:8 NKJV). May God help every Christian to believe!

Remind Archippus

The last words of Paul's letter to the Church at Colossae are easily overlooked. Readers may pass by it without giving it much thought, but it actually contains an imperative and urgent request. In Colossians 4:17,

AWAKENING THE CHURCH IN NORTH AMERICA

Paul tells the leaders in the church to remind someone named "Archippus" to be sure to fulfil the ministry he had been given by the Lord!

The Church must always remind believers of their call to minister. In fact, church pastors and leaders are charged with the ministry of "reminding" the Saints. When it comes to preaching to the church, for the most part, new messages are not what is needed, but consistent reminders of what Christians already know.

The apostle Peter took making and being a reminder seriously, declaring in 2 Peter 1:12-13: "Wherefore I will not be negligent to put you always in remembrance of these things, though ye know them, and be established in the present truth. Yea, I think it meet, as long as I am in this tabernacle, to stir you up by putting you in remembrance" (KJV).

Paul's challenge to remind Archippus of what matters most is compelling. If Christians are awakened to the ministry received from the Lord, it will affect everything else in their lives! It will move their attention to being disciples and to their calling in the mission of the Church. They will invest themselves in building the kingdom of God and edifying the church. Just imagine the change it will make for every true believer to take to heart Jesus'

"Rise Up, O Church of God"

charge in John 20:21: "As the Father has sent Me, I also send you" (NKJV). Outreach then becomes their passion and evangelistic zeal becomes the new church culture when church members are laser-focused on fulfilling the ordained purpose Jesus gave in John 15:16: "I have chosen you, and ordained you . . . that ye should go and bring forth fruit" (KJV).

Paul didn't say "give" Archippus a title or job description. He said to remind Archippus of the ministry *he had received of the Lord*. There are many who need help in clarifying their ministry. For example, few things are more important than Christians remembering their call to ministry from the Lord. Every Christian has been given the ministry of reconciliation. The pastoral message of 2 Corinthians 5:20, which reminds believers they are called to be ambassadors of Christ in the world, is both wanted and desperately needed.

Church members and regular attenders know they are called, but it is as if the church gave them a free pass. Unless every Christian takes responsibility for his or her own ministry, there will be no positive change in the Church. Christians need regular reminders that the Holy Spirit teaches, guides, and clothes Christ-followers with special power to be witnesses.

AWAKENING THE CHURCH IN NORTH AMERICA

Pastors and church leaders must do more than equip the saints to be good church members; sanctified and satisfied. The Biblical charge is to equip them to be missionaries here and now! The Church is a movement that believes in the priesthood of all believers . . . regardless of where their paycheck originates.

Do not be guilty of talking about the harvest in abstract terms; it is more than just a concept. Do not say it is somewhere in the future—another place, another time, for another day. The harvest is every day and in every place unsaved people are found. Christians are His witnesses. Christians are salt and light at their jobs, in conversation among their daily contacts and casual acquaintances, in schools, and in the marketplace. If there is to be a great awakening in your community, it will be through the "priesthood of all believers"—men and women who are "reminded" to fulfill the ministry they have received of the Lord.

Paul wasn't being mysterious by calling the church to remind Archippus. Ultimately, everyone's ministry moves toward the same goalpost. As Jesus said to the disciples in John chapter 4, after ministering to the woman at the well: Just look . . . here is your ministry opportunity. What they

"RISE UP, O CHURCH OF GOD"

most likely saw coming was a great number of Samaritans. They probably saw men and women dressed in traditional white clothing, that were following the woman at the well. Jesus told them to lift up their eyes and look. He knew people get too self-absorbed. Jesus was suggesting that, even though the disciples didn't personally know these people, they were being called to reap where they had not labored. He was saying to them, and to the Church today, "Don't look at yourself, look for the obvious opportunity." Encourage everyone you know to start reaping the harvest right now, no matter where they are.

To have a successful harvest, *seeders* alone are not enough; *reapers* are also necessary. On the Day of Pentecost, the world harvest was in the streets of Jerusalem. They were described as "learned people from the known world were gathered" (see Acts 2:5-11). To those gathered, 120 Spirit-filled harvest reapers flowed out of the Upper Room, speaking in tongues as the Spirit gave them utterance. They had nothing to do with sowing that harvest, but they had everything to do with reaping it.

The needed awakening is one of reaping the harvest regardless of when, where, or how it is encountered. Christians must lift up their eyes, look for the harvest, and reap it.

Vision Is Revealed in Prayer Requests

Dr. Tom Rainer, a long-time and highly respected church researcher, suggests that the lack of evangelism in the Church is not a failure of methodology, but of spiritual obedience. Unfortunately, the Great Commission is currently less than compelling when 57 percent of Christian Millennials believe it is wrong to evangelize.

Perhaps the key to awakening each community to the gospel of the Kingdom is the people in each local church. An authentic spiritual awakening is only accomplished by the Holy Spirit. Therefore, churches need more than updated methodology, restructured systems, new signage, and modernized style in their sanctuaries. Awakenings begin with sincere repentance of spiritual apathy and blindness to the ripened harvest. Becoming a Spirt-filled church requires taking a posture of humility, soul searching, rethinking processes, but more than anything else, prayer—heart-rending prayer. Awakenings require praying until true direction from the Holy Spirit is received. Someone once said, "You can tell a lot about people by listening to their prayer requests." Perhaps each believer should carefully evaluate their prayers.

God's people are challenged to pray for laborers for

"RISE UP, O CHURCH OF GOD"

the harvest. Matthew 9:37-38 says, "The harvest truly is plenteous, but the labourers are few; pray ye therefore the Lord of the harvest, that he will send forth labourers into his harvest" (KJV). Pastors should call their people to pray this prayer and to also become the answer to their own prayers by becoming laborers in the harvest. Too many Christians pray for God to work while ignoring His call for them to work as well! Some pray for God to move: "Oh Lord, do it again," yet fail to pray to do His work in their communities.

The challenge for the Church is to not replace the call of God's people to minister. The church was never meant to be a substitute or an alternative for Christian obedience. Christians do not fulfill their ministry only by participating

> **Christians do not fulfill their ministry only by participating inside the walls of the church.**

inside the walls of the church. The church must awaken believers and equip them for their ministry outside the church and into the harvest.

Sleeping Giants

When someone is sound asleep, they are not aware of anything. They are not cognizant of potential threats

AWAKENING THE CHURCH IN NORTH AMERICA

or loss. The Church is filled with Christians who want to be left alone and allowed to just sleep. Speaking from years of personal observation in many churches, from north to south and east to west, way too many churches mirror the situation described in Proverbs 24: 30-34:

> I walked by the field of a certain lazy fellow and saw that it was overgrown with thorns, and covered with weeds; and its walls were broken down. Then, as I looked, I learned this lesson:
> "A little extra sleep,
> A little more slumber,
> A little folding of the hands to rest"
> means that poverty will break in upon you suddenly like a robber, and violently like a bandit (TLB).

This word picture describes a man who had no sense of purpose, but it also presents the tragic consequences of a sleeping group of church members. Some Christians have lost all sight of their purpose and calling, and frankly, some just don't care.

Not all sleeping Christians can be awakened, but some of them can. Just 2 percent of a culture can actually change an entire culture. This provides hope and makes every effort important. And, if it's true that sin is so powerful that a little leaven can infiltrate the whole loaf, and if the things impossible with men are possible

"RISE UP, O CHURCH OF GOD"

with God, and if Jesus infuses Himself whenever two or three gather in His name, then whoever will listen must be challenged.

A pastor friend once shared a dream he had about a giant on his back. He said he was alive but in a deep sleep. The pastor attempted to wake him up, but the giant remained asleep. He shook him as hard as he could, trying everything he knew, but was unable to rouse him. He felt sad that this great giant would not wake up.

You may feel that way about your church. However, don't give up—it only takes one or two giants to awaken and turn around the entire church!

Look for sleeping giants everywhere you go. They may not even be attending church at the moment. However, the Spirit works behind the scenes. You can inspire and

> **Look for sleeping giants everywhere you go.**

motivate people to become laborers wherever you are— don't give up!

2

SPIRITUAL DNA MATTERS

"But you shall receive power when the Holy Spirit has come upon you; and you shall be witnesses to Me in Jerusalem, and in all Judea and Samaria, and to the end of the earth"
(Acts 1:8 NKJV).

Although a gross oversimplification, it can be said that by evaluating DNA, we can understand how unique traits and characteristics, including physical features, and certain predispositions, can be passed from one generation to another. This is why we sometimes say, "It's in my DNA." When used in an unscientific way, the term *DNA* has been used for organizations, fraternal orders, and even churches. This suggests there are certain distinctive traits inherent in each of these that have been passed down to successive generations. It is common nomenclature to refer to such distinctives as "in our DNA."

The first doctrinal principle adopted by the Church of God was, "We believe the whole Bible, rightly divided.

The New Testament is the only rule for government and discipline." The centrality of the word is a basic concept that permeates our literature. It is "in our DNA."

It is vital to know the stories of our movement's application of the Word of God in the context of our unique *spiritual DNA*, and how this intersects with postmodern culture. Hopefully, this section will provide a better understanding and deeper appreciation for how the Word of God drives our mission and vision.

The Holy Word and the Holy Spirit

Since its inception, the Church of God has held a high regard for the Scriptures, believing that the sixty-six canonical books of both the Old and New Testaments comprise, for the Church, the very Word of God. As previously stated, the first principle adopted by the infant movement was, "The Church of God stands for the whole Bible rightly divided. The New Testament is the only rule for government and discipline." Although this position was espoused as early as 1910, in a prepared report to the General Assembly, there was no official record of the General Assembly having approved the report. Consequently, the 1930 General Assembly agreed:

SPIRITUAL DNA MATTERS

> We do now declare the laws and teachings of the Bible,
> as set forth in the report of the said committee on page
> 47 of the 1910 Minutes of the General Assembly
> under the heading 'Church of God Teachings' to be
> the official findings and interpretations of the 1930
> Assembly of the Church of God. . . .

Furthermore, with the acceptance of the Declaration of Faith at the 1948 Assembly, Article One codified the belief "in the verbal inspiration of the Bible." Thus, the centrality of the Word of God to faith and practice has long been embedded in the church's spiritual DNA.

The Church of God is not only a Word-centered church, but also its Doctrinal Commitment 8 states we believe in the "baptism with the Holy Ghost subsequent to cleansing; the enduement of power for service." While fully Pentecostal and emphasizing that speaking in tongues is the initial evidence of Spirit baptism, the Church has historically emphasized that power to become a witness to the saving grace of Christ and to the authority of the Word of God is the primary purpose for this experience. The baptism in the Holy Spirit introduces believers to the gifts of the Spirit, and this is an important dimension of our personality as a movement. This enduement of power is essential to the proper exegesis and declaration

AWAKENING THE CHURCH IN NORTH AMERICA

of the Word of God, and as such, is a tracible component of our family heritage.

As a Word-centered church, a core understanding includes the knowledge that before Jesus sent His disciples into all the world, He sent them first to the Upper Room to be endued with power (see Luke 24:49). It was this supernatural empowering that transformed a stumbling, bumbling, and sometimes backsliding Simon Peter into that powerful Pentecostal preacher recorded in Acts 2, and into perhaps one of the two most effective apostles of Jesus (the other being Paul). Prior to his Spirit baptism, Peter denied Jesus three times. After being filled with the Spirit, he proclaimed with Pentecostal power, "God has made this Jesus, whom you crucified, both Lord and Christ" (Acts 2:36 NKJV). The Spirit and the Word always agree, so it can be concluded that it is impossible to effectively declare the Word without the anointing and empowerment of the Holy Spirit.

Power for Service

James E. Cossey tells of his call to ministry and of being prematurely pressured to preach his first sermon at age fifteen, even before being baptized in the Holy Spirit. Knowing he was being called of God, he agreed to try,

SPIRITUAL DNA MATTERS

and in his words, "I felt it was a complete disaster, and vowed never to do it again." For months, while exploring schools to study broadcast journalism, the high school sophomore expressed no interest and felt no urgency or sense of calling to preach.

Then came the revival! Hungry for more of God, scores of teenagers attended, and on Wednesday night, James and several others were baptized in the Holy Spirit. The evangelist had preached on the Holy Spirit baptism as an equipping experience, an enduement of power for service. The invitation was not to come and seek tongues, but was given with an assurance that tongues would come with the enduement. It was not an invitation to come and seek gifts, but to come and seek Christ, who would equip sincere seekers with both gifts and spiritual power. Cossey says, "I was baptized in the Holy Spirit with the initial evidence of speaking with other tongues as the Spirit gave the utterance. Whereupon," he says, "I got up from the altar, and as I was walking down the aisle to leave, the Holy Spirit spoke to me clearly and said, 'Now, go preach My Gospel!'" Cossey says from that point on, "I could not 'not preach' the Gospel," which he has done now for more than fifty years.

Preaching the Word of God with Pentecostal power is in the DNA of the Church of God, which is one reason individuals must testify to having been baptized in the Holy Spirit in order to be credentialed as ministers. It is who we are! "You shall receive power when the Holy Spirit has come upon you; and you shall be witnesses to Me" (Acts 1:8 NKJV). It is not a choice of either/or. The Word without the Spirit may lead to formalism, and the Spirit without the Word may lead to fanaticism.

> **The Word without the Spirit may lead to formalism, and the Spirit without the Word may lead to fanaticism.**

A Church Transformed

Revival and revitalization occur when the Word of God meets the fire of the Holy Spirit! Herein lies the answer for the cold apathy of this generation. In the atmosphere of the Word of God, quickened by the fire of the Holy Spirit, lives are transformed, churches are revived, families are changed, and nations turn to God.

Pastor Michael Alley faced the challenge of leading a struggling church. Strife, apathy, and no vision were all characteristics of that congregation. Workers filled

SPIRITUAL DNA MATTERS

positions without passion or direction. Pastor Alley's heart cried out for revival.

While attending a Church of God General Assembly, Alley heard the call of God to get back to reading the Word. The Holy Spirit directed him to help his congregation become immersed in the Word. Upon his return to his Kokomo, Indiana, pastorate, he met with the church leadership team and shared his heart to get every member into the Word of God. They made a commitment as a congregation to read the Bible through once each month. They used varied formats for reading, even having every member read Scripture at the same time. The goal was for every person at the Kokomo church to be saturated with the Word of God. In just four years, the church members and friends have read the Scriptures through sixty-five times.

Said Pastor Alley:

The results have been astounding. Our church now has an immeasurable love for the Word. We have changed! God has done something unique in this church. Since the start of the Bible reading, people have begun to walk in their new calls of ministry. Reaching the lost has become a priority. People are saved in every service. Drug addicts and alcoholics are coming to the church where lives are changed. Apathy is gone. Strife is gone.

> The church is now known as a loving church, built on the Word of God, where lives are transformed.

The Holy Word promises us the Holy Spirit. The Holy Spirit honors the truths of the Holy Word. Thus, as Bishop David Gosnell has said, "Revival and revitalization occur when the Word of God meets the fire of the Holy Spirit!" It is in our DNA.

A Pentecostal Approach to the Great Commission

The Church of God historian, Dr. David Roebuck, provides keen insight on how our movement was birthed with a burning passion for the Great Commission. As an early pastor and the first general overseer, A. J. Tomlinson shaped the theology and ministry of the early Church of God. In his book *The Last Great Conflict*, Tomlinson reminded readers that God is love, and He demonstrates love through His works and the works of His people. Love compelled the Father to give His only begotten Son for a sinful world. Referring to this gift, Tomlinson wrote, "then love gave love." In Christ, we too obtain the fullness of God's love, which enables us to give our possessions and our lives to reach the lost. Tomlinson concluded, "This world is dying and going to

SPIRITUAL DNA MATTERS

hell for want of love. They must be loved."

Tomlinson expressed the urgency with which the church must act. A recognition of the value of souls and the reality of hell will cause any church that is half-asleep to wake up, see the harvest, and take action. Rather than shifting the responsibility to future generations, the Church must put today's resources into the harvest. Those who cannot go into the harvest should use all means available to send those who can.

When delegates to the first General Assembly in 1906 discussed the importance of fulfilling the Great Commission, they took time to consecrate themselves for the task before them. The record of that meeting reveals their passion: "After the consideration of the ripened fields and open doors for evangelism this year, strong men wept and said they were not only willing, but really anxious to go."

For the early Church of God, motivation to fulfill the Great Commission included an overwhelming sense that these were the last days. Tomlinson wrote in the inaugural issue of *The Church of God Evangel*, "The command to go, the command to evangelize is just as forcible today upon us, upon whom the ends of the world have come as it was when first uttered by our Lord and great Head of the Church." He continued, "The Holy Spirit was given to the disciples in the morning to give them power to accomplish just what they did accomplish. He is given to us today for the same purpose. We dare not falter. . . . The time is short. The harvest is ripe. The sickle must be furbished and put into use."

Connecting Joel's prophecy with the contemporary outpouring of the Holy Spirit, church pioneers saw their experience as the fulfillment of the Biblical promise of the latter rain. The outpouring of the Spirit on the Day of Pentecost was for planting God's church, and the outpouring of the Spirit in these last days is to reap the final harvest before the Lord's return.

Tomlinson wrote that it will be those who go "back to Pentecost" that the Holy Spirit will equip to reach the last-days harvest. First, the Holy Spirit enables believers to speak about Jesus. Tomlinson reminded his readers of the words of Jesus, "But when the Comforter is come, whom I will send unto you from the Father, even the Spirit of truth, which proceedeth from the Father, he shall testify of me" (John 15:26 KJV). Along with Spirit empowered-speech, returning back to Pentecost includes

SPIRITUAL DNA MATTERS

the restoration of the apostles' doctrine and fellowship, along with manifestations of signs and wonders. The results will be a supernatural spread of the Gospel.

Desiring to see growth, the young movement used a variety of means and methods. The first Assembly recommended Sunday schools as an effective way to plant churches. They noted, "We believe a Sunday school may sometimes be organized and run successfully where a church could not be established at once, thereby opening and paving the way for more permanent work in the future."

The early Pentecostal church did not depend on church buildings. Few communities had facilities sufficient to establish a church or conduct a building campaign, so they often utilized brush arbors and tents on borrowed property. They could construct brush arbors quickly, and tents were a practical and portable way to provide inexpensive shelter for services.

Historical author Kenneth O. Brown has shown how tents provided social and psychological space to hear the Gospel. It was easier to attend a meeting outside one's own tradition if the setting was not a local church. Additionally, the uniqueness of a tent service held one's

AWAKENING THE CHURCH IN NORTH AMERICA

attention, and the excitement allowed worshippers to expect and be open to the new and unusual. Tomlinson wrote in his journal on June 22, 1908: "Have been in a tent meeting in Chattanooga. . . . Closed there last night after a siege of seven weeks. . . . People would stay for hours and sit on the rough boards with no backs, when they could hardly be kept an hour on nice comfortable pews in the churches."

Often, local churches planted missions in nearby communities that they sought to reach with the Gospel. Soon after Tomlinson established the North Cleveland Church of God in 1906, the congregation immediately began to look for places to plant churches. Within months, they were holding tent meetings in surrounding communities. They held tent meetings, sent workers, and provided finances. In 1910, they built a tabernacle to reach the southern part of the city. Their work led to the organization of the South Cleveland Church of God—a strong congregation in the growing city.

Fulfilling the Great Commission was not primarily the work of credentialed ministers, as every Christian was encouraged to put their sickle into the harvest. Tomlinson challenged the General Assembly in 1911, "We have

SPIRITUAL DNA MATTERS

a number of workers who are not able to preach but are willing to work at anything they can do. They are able to do personal work, hold cottage prayer meetings, distribute literature, and give ringing testimonies." Indeed, it was often only after a small group of people were worshiping together that a minister joined them to set a church in order.

On one occasion while serving as general overseer, Ray H. Hughes, in reflecting on the early days of the Church of God, said that people were often heard to say, "Let's go down to that Church where *all the people* preach!" His reflections spoke of the desire of every member to share the Word of God whenever and wherever they had an opportunity, both formally and informally.

It has been said that 60 percent of church members today do not feel sharing their faith with others is an essential obligation of their Christian life; 75 percent do not feel personal witnessing is required of them; and more than 90 percent have never led an unsaved person to faith in Christ.

A family DNA characteristic of the Church of God is passion for evangelism—a burning desire to see lost souls coming to Christ and born into the kingdom of God.

> **A family DNA characteristic of the Church of God is passion for evangelism— a burning desire to see lost souls coming to Christ and born into the kingdom of God.**

As the first general overseer and others have since emphasized, the effort and burden of evangelism have never been historically viewed as specialty ministries reserved for people with those particular ministry gifts, but rather were seen as the responsibility of all believers. Similar to the model of the New Testament church in the Book of Acts, the Church of God has long labored to foster what author Ed Stetzer calls "a culture of evangelistic accountability." Without a doubt, this was a great contributing factor in our early growth and expansion.

Urgency Drives the Church Forward

The Church of God has always been driven by a sense of urgency for the harvest, propelled by the belief in the imminent return of Jesus. The second coming of Christ is a foundational doctrine. The Declaration of Faith declares belief in the premillennial second coming of Jesus. The urgency of reaching a last-days harvest is illustrated by the words of Jesus, "I must work the works

SPIRITUAL DNA MATTERS

of Him who sent Me while it is day; the night is coming when no one can work" (John 9:4 NKJV). The phrase "while it is day" gives emphasis to the urgency of the call on believers to reach a global harvest that begins in our own family, community, and nation. "He who testifies to these things says, 'Surely I am coming quickly.' Amen. Even so, come, Lord Jesus!" (Rev. 22:20 NKJV).

Jesus conveyed the sense of urgency for the harvest in the parable of the great banquet:

> Then He said to him, "A certain man gave a great supper and invited many, and sent his servant at supper time to say to those who were invited, 'Come, for all things are now ready.' But they all with one accord began to make excuses. . . . That servant came and reported these things to his master. Then the master of the house, being angry, said to his servant, 'Go out quickly into the streets and lanes of the city, and bring in here the poor and the maimed and the lame and the blind.' And the servant said, 'Master, it is done as you commanded, and still there is room.' Then the master said to the servant, 'Go out into the highways and hedges, and compel them to come in, that my house may be filled'" (Luke 14:16-23 NKJV).

Writing to his spiritual son Timothy, the apostle Paul issued the challenge, "Never lose your sense of urgency, in season or out of season. Prove, correct, and encourage,

AWAKENING THE CHURCH IN NORTH AMERICA

using the utmost patience in your teaching" (2 Tim. 4:2 Ph.). Without a sense of urgency, the church loses one of its core motivations. Imbedded in our DNA, this sense of urgency has helped propel the church and enabled it to progress from a humble regional movement of sincere mountain believers to a worldwide ministry literally circling the globe!

Perhaps it was this same sense of urgency that compelled Philip the Evangelist to leave an explosive Holy Spirit outpouring in Samaria (see Acts 8) where three thousand souls were saved to go down a desert road between Jerusalem and Gaza. There in the desert, he would stumble upon an Ethiopian eunuch, lead him to Christ, and baptize him in water. Philip probably never realized the impact of that moment, perhaps even questioning why God would move him from a fertile Gospel revival in a major city out into the desert; but history shows us that this Ethiopian eunuch is likely the seed that germinated the Gospel in Africa with the Christians of that continent now tracing the origins of their faith back to this moment.

Urgency about God's work has always directed the Church's plans. "For He says: 'In an acceptable time I have heard you, and in the day of salvation I have helped

SPIRITUAL DNA MATTERS

you.' Behold, now is the accepted time; behold, now is the day of salvation" (2 Cor. 6:2 NKJV). It was Jesus who said, "Do you not say, 'There are still four months and then comes the harvest'? Behold, I say to you, lift up your eyes and look at the fields, for they are already white for harvest" (John 4:35 NKJV).

Responding to this sense of urgency has resulted in many Christ-followers leaving a crowd of friends in their rearview mirror—sometimes friends who cannot understand why one would forsake all to be faithful to the Great Commission, and at other times, friends who cheer, encourage, and support as the work of God progresses. Historically, pioneering men and women in every generation since the inception of the Church of God have found their greatest fulfillment in knowing they are obedient to the call of God, and that they are part of a legacy that will remind future generations not only of their faithfulness to God, but of God's faithfulness to them! It's in our DNA!

In his 1973 publication, *Look Out! The Pentecostals are Coming,* C. Peter Wagner chronicled the growth and expansion of the Pentecostal Movement in Latin America, of which the Church of God is an integral

AWAKENING THE CHURCH IN NORTH AMERICA

part. Wagner's assertion was that every Pentecostal believer in Latin America, although not credentialed or ordained, was a proclaimer of the gospel of Christ. Wagner connected this observation to the fact that Latin American Pentecostals were so committed to the Word of God and so full of the power of the Holy Spirit that they could not keep the message to themselves; they were compelled to share it with others. This compulsion led to the development of Sunday schools, Bible studies, and new church plants wherever a nucleus of people could be gathered.

According to research, literally tens of millions of Latin Americans have left the Roman Catholic Church in recent decades and embraced Pentecostal Christianity. Multitudes of others, who could only be classified as unbelievers, have seen what is happening among family and friends and have turned to Christ and to the Pentecostal Movement. As many as one in five Latin Americans in countries once dominated by Catholicism now describe themselves as Protestant, and across the surveyed countries of Latin America and Puerto Rico, majorities of these identify as Pentecostal or belonging to a Pentecostal denomination.

As one reads Charles W. Conn's historical accounts

SPIRITUAL DNA MATTERS

of the Church of God in *Like a Mighty Army,* and in other histories of the earliest days of the Pentecostal outpouring in North America, one readily sees the similarity between what occurred then and what is happening now in places like Latin America, Asia, and Africa.

The challenge for today is to seriously reevaluate our denominational DNA in an all-out effort to rediscover and fully appreciate who we are as a movement. Our DNA declares that the word for today is for us to fully commit to continue to be a Bible-based, Pentecostal people who are motivated by our mission to truly finish the Great Commission in the Spirit and power of Pentecost!

Collaborative Team Members for "Spiritual DNA Matters"

James Cossey, Collaborative Coach
Director, Paraclete Coaching and Consulting

Michael Alley
Senior Pastor, Woodland Church of God,
Kokomo, Indiana

David Gosnell
Administrative Bishop, Church of God, Indiana

Travis Johnson
Lead Pastor, Pathway Church of God,
Mobile, Alabama
Executive Director, People for Care and Learning

William Lee Jr.
International Evangelist and Urban Ministries,
Church of God, Cleveland, Tennessee

Gary Lewis
Administrative Bishop, Church of God,
South Georgia

David Roebuck
Director, Lee University Pentecostal Research Center,
Church Historian, Cleveland, Tennessee

3

REVIVING WHAT REMAINS

"Thus says the Lord of hosts, 'Consider your ways! Go up to the mountains and bring wood and build the temple, that I may take pleasure in it and be glorified,' says the Lord"
(Haggai 1:7-8 NKJV).

Restoring Church Health and Rebuilding for the Future

It is commonly known that the Church in North America is in decline. Most Pentecostal movements were birthed out of a desire to experience more of God. Concentrated prayer, Holy Spirit empowerment, and a commitment to reading the Word of God resulted in spiritual renewal and a revitalized church. Church planting, renewal, and revitalization are in the spiritual DNA of almost all Pentecostal movements.

In the postexilic atmosphere of rebuilding the city of Jerusalem, God's people had rebuilt the walls and the gates leading into the city. They were even in the process of rebuilding their homes. The Lord spoke to them and said, "Thus says the Lord of hosts, 'Consider your ways! Go up to the mountains and bring down wood and build the temple, that I may take pleasure in it and be glorified,' says the Lord" (Haggai 1:7-8 NKJV). Perhaps now, more than ever is a good time for the Church in North America to also consider her ways. How healthy is the Church? How successful is the Church at reaching the harvest, making disciples, and planting life-giving churches?

In Revelation 3:1-2, Jesus said to the church at Sardis, "You have a name that you are alive, but you are dead. Be watchful, and strengthen the things which remain" (NKJV). It was a wakeup call for the church. The good news is that local churches, and the church in North America, do not have to die. It is certainly a good time to "be watchful, and strengthen the things which remain" (v. 2). The mordern terminology for this process is church revitilization. The simple definition is, "to restore new life and vitality to something that was vital and vibrant but is now in decline." Revitalization is an ongoing process of restoring church health and reviving what remains with the purpose of reaping the Lord's harvest.

Successful church revitalization means prayerfully following these steps:

- **Respect** the past.
- **Reassess** the current reality.
- **Re-vision** for the future.
- **Re-strategize**
- **Realign** ministries to fit mission and vision.
- **Rebrand** if necessary.

1. Respect

Pastors of existing churches should respect and care for their members while determining the condition of their church. Changes may be needed, but they should be approached in a thoughtful, systematic process.

Many pastors feel their appointment or selection as the pastor gives them the right to immediately make arbitrary changes. Every church has a story, a history, a personality that defines and describes it. Respect for the traditions, policies, practices, memories, and feelings people have about those things is crucial when leading change. This attitude of "there is a new sheriff in town" usually ends up in disaster. When untethered change is initiated, members may become discouraged and disengage from serving in the church.

Pastor Jason Daughdrill, who is experiencing great success in revitalizing an older congregation in Shelbyville,

AWAKENING THE CHURCH IN NORTH AMERICA

Tennessee, told the faithful members, "We will revitalize this church on your shoulders, not in your face. We will not frame our future by discrediting our past." This pastor honored and respected the past but encouraged the people not to stay stuck in the past. Honor demands leaders, and pastors lead change with wisdom, new energy, zeal *and* respect.

> "We will revitalize this church on your shoulders, not in your face. We will not frame our future by discrediting our past."

2. Reassess

Revitalization involves reassessing ministries to diagnose the true health of the church. The church at Sardis had a reputation that they were alive but, in fact, Jesus said, "You are dead. Be watchful, and strengthen the things which remain" (Revelation 3:1-2 NKJV). The church needs to celebrate strengths and nurture the things being done right. When ministers and members assess the true condition of the church, it reveals areas that need to be repaired and revitalized. Good assessment tools can provide a better picture of how to bring the church back to good health. One of these great tools for determining church health is the Church Health Survey, which takes the pulse of the local church.

Some twenty-eight years ago, David Smith became the pastor of a declining congregation of twelve people in Pueblo, Colorado. He determined to strengthen, value, and build up the people who remained. He accepted the current reality of his church rather than despise it. As he discipled those God gave him to pastor, he helped them discover their strengths and spiritual gifts, and released them as a spiritual team to make more followers of Jesus. Both "respect" and "reassessment" were key revitalization principles that helped grow this church into a large, vibrant ministry in Pueblo.

Reassessing the current reality can put churches on the pathway to good health as they strengthen what remains.

3. Re-vision

A clear understanding of mission and vision must be presented to the congregation by the lead pastor. Mission and vision must be at the forefront of everything that is done. The mission is really very simple: Win the lost to Christ and disciple them to follow Him faithfully. The vision typically begins with a burden over something that

Awakening the Church in North America

needs to be done. This burden causes people to pray and seek God for a solution. Prayer usually provides the vision to see what needs to be done. Vision is a clear picture of a desired future.

When Nehemiah heard of the sad and oppressed condition of God's people in Jerusalem, he began to fast, pray, and cry out to God for several months. As he continued to pray, he envisioned the broken-down walls being rebuilt. It was a picture embedded in his spirit and mind of a rebuilt city and a revitalized people. Nehemiah couldn't get away from it. The burden and the clear vision were compelling. If a leader has a clear vision and he communicates it well to the people, they will follow that lead. This is also based on a track record of the leader making right decisions over an extended period of time.

Another pastor who assumed leadership of a declining church, Sam Santana (Tucson, Arizona), soon realized there was a lack of trust of leadership. This lack of trust was slowing progress and growth. Distrust of leadership resulted in lack of enthusiasm, low attendance, and challenging financial issues. He determined that a pastor must always maintain a high level of integrity in relationships, finances, ministry, and family. Pastor Santana and his wife lived and led the church members and friends this way for years and eventually built a very strong, healthy, and large congregation.

When pastors live with integrity and demonstrate Christ-honoring character, they earn the right to lead congregations to do greater things. Then, when the vision is communicated clearly, the congregation will follow. Whatever gets talked about frequently is the thing most likely to get done. For the future of the church, effective leaders must keep the mission and vision in front of the people by talking about it often.

Mitchell Tolle is an amazing artist by profession and was asked to pastor a declining church in Kentucky. He had taught Sunday school for many years as a layman but was new to serving as a pastor. He accepted the assignment, and the church's story of revitalization is an amazing work of God's grace. Pastor Tolle cites three reasons for this successful church revitalization:

1. We knew we were in the will of God.

2. We redeemed all that was good and honored the past.

3. We saw, or had a vision, of the end result from the beginning.

Almost everyone knows the words of Solomon, "Where there is no vision, the people perish" (Prov. 29:18 KJV). Vision gives fuel for a dying church to come alive with God's presence.

4. Re-strategize

It is true: "Where there is no vision, the people [will] perish" (Proverbs 29:18 KJV), but it is also true where there is no strategy, the vision will perish. As Nehemiah fasted, prayed, and received a vision from God, he also developed a strategy to accomplish the vision.

When, one day, the king asked Nehemiah why he was so sad, he had a response ready: "Why shouldn't I look sad when the city, the place where my ancestors are buried, is in ruins and its gates are burned down?" (Nehemiah 2:3 GW). When the king asked, "What do you want?" (v. 4), Nehemiah was able to lay out his strategy, and the king granted all his requests. When God is the author of the vision, He often grants the requests of His servants.

As a young pastor, J. J. Chiara assumed the pastorate of a small, older church in Pennsylvania, and developed a three-step strategy:

1. Create an environment for change.
2. Have a clear vision for the future of the church.

3. Discover areas for "quick wins."

The church experienced significant growth spiritually, numerically, and financially. Obviously, some changes happened more in the long-term than in the short-term. Re-strategizing may mean rethinking the potential influence and impact of modern-day revival. The Pentecostal movement is classically known for having some of the greatest preachers who ever stepped into a pulpit.

Times have changed, and the revival climate is much different today. Some would even say revivals and evangelists—in the traditional sense of the words—are a thing of the past. Evangelists strongly believe their ministries are relevant and ordained by God. Drawing from Ephesians 4:11, "He Himself gave some to be apostles, some prophets, some evangelists, and some pastors and teachers" (NKJV), each of them shares the certainty of their call and the strong conviction that God still plans to use them for revival in these last days.

Evangelist Michael Ball of Eastern North Carolina explained:

> This is my calling—this is where God has me. There is
> a passion inside of me, a drive. It does get wearisome
> at times, being away from my family and enduring the
> toll it takes on my body, but this is what God has called

AWAKENING THE CHURCH IN NORTH AMERICA

me to do. If I were to do anything else at this juncture of my life, I would be out of God's will.

The words, "the call," are prevalent in conversations with evangelists. Larry Timmerman loves evangelism and shares a particularly touching account of his call.

> My being an evangelist basically goes back to when I was five years old. My dad took me to an Oral Roberts crusade in Charlotte, North Carolina. We sat down on the front row and I watched as Oral Roberts sat down in a chair and started praying for people. They brought a little boy up for prayer, about eight or nine years old, who was totally crippled. My father and I saw that child miraculously healed that night. I remember looking up at my father and saying, "I want to do that." In my mind I go back to that night often because I still want to see people healed spiritually, physically, and emotionally. My whole drive in a revival is to minister to those needs. This is what I am called to do.

Revival looked much different twenty-five years ago than it does today. It used to be very common for a pastor to schedule two or three revivals per year. Those revivals were at least a week in length, with some meetings extending beyond that. Today, if revivals are scheduled at all, they are usually Sunday through Wednesday. Some churches have chosen to designate a Sunday as "Revival

REVIVING WHAT REMAINS

Sunday" with an evangelist invited to preach. Although change is inevitable, the men and women called to lead revival feel the church is missing an opportunity to impact lives and affect a community.

"Things have changed a great deal from when I started," said Jacqueline Smith, who has been evangelizing more than forty years. She explains:

When I began, church had first place in people's lives. They looked forward to coming to revival and making the sacrifice to be a part of it. Revivals would start out for one week, and when people would get saved and filled with the Holy Spirit, we would decide to go on for another week. I have preached in revivals for up to three consecutive weeks, but that has all changed now. People are involved in so many different things, making it difficult for them to come out for a weeklong revival. As a result, pastors have concluded the people won't come out, so they don't schedule revivals. A church may have weekend services and call it a "Power Weekend" or just have two services on Sunday and call it a "Day of Refreshing." I really believe if pastors would go ahead and schedule the meetings—and things happened in those meetings—people would still support revival.

Many evangelists agree scheduling and conducting revivals today is far different from when they began their

87

AWAKENING THE CHURCH IN NORTH AMERICA

ministries. However, there is a common optimism for the future of revival in the Church.

Clifton West, who has been an evangelist in Virginia since he was a teenager, said:

> I do think there is hope. I think the best way to promote revival in the future is to have revival in the present. In other words, if someone really experiences revival, they must value it. I'm not talking about a revival in name—just a series of services—we've had plenty of that. I'm talking about a revival that is transformational; people will still value that!"

Revival is part of the DNA of the Church of God. Evangelists have played a key role in what God has done in this movement from the very beginning. Because it is part of the fivefold ministry listed in Ephesians 4, it will remain a vital tool for Kingdom advancement for the times to come. Younger people are buying in and finding their place in the move of God in their generation. There is reason to be optimistic for the future.

Jacqueline Smith sees a new season emerging. She shares:

> I'm beginning to see a hunger again and it's starting with the younger ones. This is why I can't stop. The young people need me. This is how I explain it—Elizabeth and Mary were pregnant at the same time;

REVIVING WHAT REMAINS

they were both productive and fruitful simultaneously. We need to do this together—we need each other. Elizabeth could have developed an attitude and said, 'I've been here longer; I should be the one carrying the Messiah.' But she didn't do that. Her role was to give life to the forerunner; younger Mary delivered Jesus. They each were important. They helped each other, loved each other, and celebrated together. This attitude will bring great revival to the church today!

Revival and evangelists—these words may be considered old-fashioned by some, but they still carry a glimmer of hope for a church that God is calling to rise up and declare the good news of the Gospel to a dying world. While some in the church are choosing to stir the ashes of a former revival, God is still anointing men and women to spread the fresh fire of revival to hungry hearts today. It may look different from the past, but it is happening—evangelists are being used by God. Revival is His plan and His idea, and it is indispensable to an awakening in North America and the world.

> **It may look different from the past, but it is happening— evangelists are being used by God.**

5. Realign

In many cases, churches have not kept the pace with a mission and vision for the future, putting them out of alignment with God's plan for the church. The church exists to take the Gospel to every person, so they have opportunity to know Jesus as their Lord and Savior. Many pastors were trained to preach sermons, but few were trained to evangelize the lost and to disciple them, which can create an imbalance.

Author Stephen Covey said, "Keep the main thing the main thing." When a telescope is out of focus, vision is not clear. When vision is not clear, people can't see where they are going. When things are out of alignment, nothing works right.

Matthew 9:35-38 says:

> Jesus went about all the cities and villages, teaching in their synagogues, preaching the gospel of the kingdom, and healing every sickness and every disease among the people. But when He saw the multitudes, He was moved with compassion for them, because they were weary and scattered, like sheep having no shepherd. Then He said to His disciples, "The harvest truly is plentiful, but the laborers are few. Therefore pray the Lord of the harvest to send out laborers into His harvest" (NKJV).

Jesus focused on the heartfelt needs of the multitude that were "scattered like sheep with no shepherd" (see v. 36). They were dysfunctional, depressed, oppressed, and had no hope for the future. However, Jesus was moved with compassion for them, and He healed them of all kinds of sicknesses and diseases.

Jesus also said, "The harvest truly is plentiful, but the laborers are few. Therefore pray the Lord of the harvest to send out laborers into His harvest" (vv. 37-38 NKJV). At first glance, it may have seemed like Jesus changed the subject away from the problems of all the struggling people. However, He was really pointing out that the harvest is truly found in the brokenness of the people. He saw the emptiness of their souls and brought healing and eternal life. Good leaders understand that priorities must be realigned to minister healing, salvation, and deliverance to those who don't know Christ.

Twenty-three years ago, Larry Hasmatali and his wife, Connie, became the pastors of thirty-five hurting adults and children in Moose Jaw, Saskatchewan, Canada. The church had declined from 185 to 35 in attendance. The newly-appointed pastor realized his first job was not to cast vision, but rather, to develop

AWAKENING THE CHURCH IN NORTH AMERICA

trust by loving and nurturing these families. The people were hurting, and they needed the time and care of a shepherd to heal and restore broken relationships. The congregation responded well to this phase of healing as the pastor shaped a new culture. Today, that church has grown to 800 spiritually healthy adherents with 600 in attendance each week! Things had to realign before real growth could occur.

6. Rebrand

Sometimes culture has changed so drastically that what the church is doing is irrelevant. Ministries must learn to contextualize the media and methods utilized by today's culture to communicate the Gospel message to them. Many times, Christians use language and methods they think unchurched people understand, but those words and methods are no longer effective. Slogans and mission statements are developed that churches think are meaningful, but they are not understood or embraced by those the church hopes to reach.

In some situations, it is helpful for a church to rebrand itself. A brand says something about who or what the church is. At times, churches may be unintentionally guilty of false advertising. Some churches use slogans such as, "The friendliest church in town." However, when evaluated by outsiders who have visited churches, members discovered they were friendly with a few close friends but were not so friendly to their guests!

A church brand is not what a church *says* they are, but it is actually what they *do* and how others perceive them to be. A church brand should encompass the mission and vision of the congregation.

7. Risk Management

Hearing from God and trusting what He says takes the risk out of faith steps. The mission is clear: Win the lost to Christ and disciple them to follow Him faithfully. When Moses sent twelve men into Canaan to spy out the land, it was not to find out whether conquest was possible; he sent them to discover how God would do the impossible. God gives impossible assignments so believers can learn to cry out to Him and to trust Him for the needed miracle. Our part is to trust, believe, and obey Him. The victory is God's, and His people enjoy the fruit of the victory.

Amy McGlamery and her husband, Kevin, pastor in Huntsville, Alabama. Amy asked Kevin about the possibility of selling the church properties of their older, well-known church. His faith-filled, unforgettable response was, "What if we fail to take a risk for God? We have always been extra-safe people. I don't want to get down the road, look back, and see that we missed our opportunity to step out in obedience." The couple took the necessary steps to sell, and the church sold in just eighteen months. For many months after, they had to be a mobile church. Their fundamental scripture for that season was, "For we walk by faith, not by sight" (2 Cor. 5:7 NKJV).

In time, the Lord provided a 75,000 square-foot building for Life Church in Huntsville. Pastor Kevin said:

> Our heavenly Father did something in our church that could only be done through our stepping out in faith. We have experienced growth in numbers, salvations, baptisms, had greater outreach, and have a renewed calling as a church to love, reach, and serve. We took the risk to step out in faith . . . and our God, who honors obedience was faithful to lead us exactly where He wanted us to be.

God gave them instructions and wisdom to successfully manage the risks.

8. Relaunch

Churches that need revitalization typically need a real

turnaround. Things may be in a downward trend for a while before the pastor and the church realize it. Often, by the time the decision is made to make necessary changes, it is late in the game. Unless things turn around quickly, the church will close. Over 4,000 churches permanently close their doors each year. A sign on the doors of one denominational headquarters church in New York said, "Out of business. We forgot what our business was!" The good news is, not every church has to die this way.

The relaunch success of a church comes down to leadership. Turnaround leadership is driven by a discovery process of assessing the strengths, weaknesses, opportunities, and threats (SWOT) of the local church. Successful church turnarounds must be led by the pastor. Pastors must lead with wisdom and vision coming from times of fervent prayer.

There are several revitalization models that assess the health of the church. God intended for the church to be a vital, life-giving body of believers. These models look at systems such as prayer ministries, worship, evangelism, discipleship, fellowship/connectivity, and serving ministries, both inside and outside the church. Another essential area to consider is leadership development. As the level of church leadership goes higher, everything in the church functions at a higher level.

Many pastors just don't know what to do, but, like the sons of Issachar who had "understanding of the times and knew what Israel ought to do" (see 1 Chronicles 12:32), leaders can hear from God to see a God-led church turnaround.

A pastor of a rural church in the North Carolina mountains, Michael Nations, points out, "Revitalization is situational and contextual, so it looks different from place to place." Smaller churches are a great part of the work of God today. The word *small* describes the size of church attendance, but *not* it's value. *Small* is not disqualifying or determinative. The point is, a revitalized small church can be a healthy, life-giving church.

> **"Revitalization is situational and contextual, so it looks different from place to place."**

As a pastor and church implement the steps in this process, they can relaunch the church with fresh, renewed vision and passion. Older congregations are actually like old wells that need to be redug. In Genesis 26, Isaac heard from God and redug the old wells his father, Abraham, had dug a generation before. He found fresh running water that was desperately needed in a time of famine. The fresh running water is symbolic of a fresh move of God.

Pastors who are willing to *risk* their reputation to follow God, are good candidates to *revitalize* and *relaunch* the church by partnering with the church leadership team and the Holy Spirit. Pastors and leaders must dare to dream, pray for a vision, and strategize. The God of all grace can bless that effort and restore church health.

AWAKENING THE CHURCH IN NORTH AMERICA

Collaborative Team Members for
"Reviving What Remains"

Mitch Maloney, Collaborative Coach
Director, USA Missions, Church of God International
Offices, Cleveland, Tennessee

Michael Ball
Evangelist, LaGrange, North Carolina

J. J. Chiara
Lead Pastor, River of God Church,
Easton, Pennsylvania

Jason Daughdrill
Lead Pastor, Gateway Church, Shelbyville, Tennessee

Larry Hasmatali
Administrative Bishop, Church of God,
Western Canada
Lead Pastor, Moose Jaw Saskatchewan, Canada

Les Higgins
Executive Administrator, USA Missions, Church of
God International Offices, Cleveland, Tennessee

Amy McGlamery
Discipleship Pastor, Life Church, Huntsville, Alabama

Michael Nations
Pastor, Clyde Church of God, Clyde, North Carolina
Founding Director, Vital Initiative, Clyde, North Carolina

Samuel Santana
Administrative Bishop, Church of God, Southwest
Hispanic Region, Upland, California

David Smith
Lead Pastor, Family Worship Center, Pueblo, Colorado

Jacqueline Smith
National Evangelist, Church of God,
Cleveland, Tennessee

Larry Timmerman
Evangelist, Church of God, Cleveland, Tennessee

Mitchell Tolle
Lead Pastor, Man O War Church of God,
Lexington, Kentucky

Clifton West
Virginia State Evangelist, Prince George, Virginia

4

PROACTIVE IN POST-CHRISTIAN CULTURE

"Of the sons of Issachar who had understanding of the times, to know what Israel ought to do, their chiefs were two hundred; and all their brethren were at their command"
(1 Chronicles 12:32 NKJV).

In recent years, life has changed, and transformation of our world has happened—from simple to complex, from assured outcomes to a world in which certainty is uncertain. Through these times of change, followers of Jesus Christ have perhaps had a difficult time making the transition into a new world, while still striving to fulfill the Great Commission of Jesus Christ. Somewhere along the way, the popular culture of the 1950s lost its wholesomeness through the significant events of the Sexual Revolution; emergence of drug culture; the Vietnam Conflict; Roe v Wade; political and spiritual leadership failures; the emergence of the LGBTQ agenda; 9/11; and the ensuing war on terror. Society

AWAKENING THE CHURCH IN NORTH AMERICA

in North America has shifted to become postmodern and even post-Christian. This shift presents a significant opportunity for the Church now and in the days ahead.

We are in a post-Christian culture, so the Gospel messenger must be a missionary—communicating Jesus Christ among people who have not heard the Gospel or do not have enough information about the Gospel to make an informed decision to accept or reject Jesus Christ.

> **The day of the missionary church has arrived, and it is the only church that will succeed.**

Writing in a prophetic manner in 1990, Kennon Callahan suggested the day of the professional pastor was over, and the day of the missionary pastor was here. Taking Callahan's thought a step further is the step the Church must take today. The day of the missionary church has arrived, and it is the only church that will succeed.

Missionary churches pray for the world to be transformed by the power of the Gospel, evangelize people by engaging them with the Gospel message, and make disciples by guiding women and men into the life-changing journey of following Jesus Christ. Although

PROACTIVE IN POST-CHRISTIAN CULTURE

taking the Gospel and fulfilling the Great Commission of Jesus Christ to go into the world and make disciples should be the most significant mission of the Church, many people find it difficult to accomplish this mission in a 21st-century world.

Jesus told the disciples to observe that the harvest was ready (see John 4:35). The United States is now the third-largest mission field in the world. It is a secular nation, with a minimal percentage of the more than 326 million people attending church on Sunday. This secularization of a nation is not uncommon or new. The continent of Europe has experienced its own secularization journey with similarities now surfacing in North America.

In addition to the challenges of the secularization of America, the American population today includes more than 488 cultural/ethnic groups, as well as six generations of people (Centenarian, Builder, Boomer, Gen X, Millennial, and Generation Z), each having significant sociological differences. This diverse context is the harvest field; and this field offers great challenges for soulwinning, evangelism, and discipleship. In order to meet these challenges, the development of strategy as well as an understanding of context are essential.

Understanding context provides opportunities for the development of relationships. Key questions frame an understanding of the harvest field and the making of disciples. Some of these questions are: What are some key characteristics of the current generation(s)? Why do I need to think, act, and minister like a cross-cultural missionary? Thinking through these questions presents important opportunities for ministry. The current and upcoming generations are the Millennials and Generation Z.

Millennials and Generation Z

Millennials (born approximately between 1981 and 1996) are slipping through the Church's fingers much like several generations before them. Millennials typically embrace experiential learning and stories. They embrace mystery and esteem relationships above all else. Since postmodern people search for truth through relationships and experiences, the best way to help them is to introduce them to Jesus! Generation Z (born approximately between 1996 and 2011) will require the church cultivating a culture of invitation and adapting methods to reach them with the Gospel.

PROACTIVE IN POST-CHRISTIAN CULTURE

Recommendations to Pastors for Reaching These Groups

Believe and act as though ministry is a cross-cultural mission field. The Church must view ministry as a missionary effort and minister as missionaries who must learn the language and customs of a "lost tribe" desperately needing the Gospel. Christians must think, act, and minister like missionaries in a foreign land.

Evaluate, adjust, and even abandon ministry methods often. While the message of the Word of God is unchanging, the *way ministry is done* must be evaluated. Methods of ministry that got the Church to where it is today are not methods that will continue to take it where it must go in the future.

The Church should focus more on "insulation," not "isolation." Several generations have slipped by while the Church built fences, dug moats, and raised drawbridges to keep the secular world out. Students and young adults cannot be hidden away from the world. They must be taught and discipled well to be insulated when they go out into the world. By finding balance between "isolation" and "insulation," the Church can better engage the spiritual hunger inside people.

Recommendations to the Church for Reaching the Groups

It is not about programs; it is about relationships. Relationships are this generation's primary delivery system of truth and values. This yearning for connection makes genuine, loving friendships into a kind of "magic wand" that opens minds and hearts to the truths of God's Word.

Learn to transform popular culture into ministry tools. Jesus used word pictures, object lessons, and parables from His culture to communicate truth. By using cultural events or things familiar to this generation in teaching and conversation, Christians can captivate listeners, opening their minds to understanding something new, like the Gospel message.

Attempt to live a balanced and Christ-centered life. Christians are watched closely. A nurturing father, a romantic married couple, or a family living within its economic means articulate more than twenty good sermons on those topics. People are not looking for someone to tell them what to do, but rather *to show them how to live.*

Studying practical ideas and concepts like these provides pastors and churches who feel less than prepared or adequate to accomplish the task, the encouragement

PROACTIVE IN POST-CHRISTIAN CULTURE

to think, create, and work to reach current generations. The pastor of a church may feel unqualified to reach the current generation. However, the responsibility remains. The local church has been, and always will be, the answer to reaching current and future generations with the love and hope found only in Jesus Christ.

> **The pastor of a church may feel unqualified to reach the current generation. However, the responsibility remains.**

As generations continue to emerge and socially evolve, and the harvest field continues to shift and change, the reality of this is not new or surprising. A quick analysis shows that what was once considered normal life practice in North America included a majority of families attending church on Sunday. The moral moorings of the Ten Commandments and the Golden Rule meant something to most people as these were taught in schools to children from a young age. Today, the world has changed, including the neighbors next door. Worldviews and social mores of the population have transformed.

Toto, We're Not in Kansas Anymore

Dr. Mark Williams, as a senior pastor, understands

the challenges of leading a large church in the changing context of society. In 2016, after twelve years of administrative service to the Church of God, Mark and Sandra Kay Williams returned to pastoral ministry. They quickly discovered how much the world has changed, as well as the social and cultural pressures that now confront the local church in its quest to make disciples.

Gone are the days of the Enlightenment. Today's world is characterized by moral relativism, rugged individualism, and privatized spirituality. Families are more diverse and technology is more accessible. Newsfeeds are filled with stories of gender fluidity, legalized marijuana, and sexual abuse. The search for Biblical truth has been replaced with the pursuit for self-fulfillment. One often hears, "Do what you want, as long as you don't get caught" or, "Believe what you want, as long as you do not hurt others." Add to this the threat of nuclear and biological terrorism, the ups and downs triggered by changes in a globalized economy, and the debate over climate change, and one can readily understand the question, "How can God be real when the world is so messed up?"

When it comes to the Church, research from highly

PROACTIVE IN POST-CHRISTIAN CULTURE

reputable agencies such as Barna Group and the Pew Foundation show a dramatic defection of nineteen- to twenty nine-year-olds from church and, in some cases, Christianity. Analysts agree that a contributing factor to this defection is a deficiency in discipleship. It seems the Church's daughters and sons were simply not prepared to meet the very real emotional or intellectual challenges to faith.

As was said of the tribe of Issachar in the Chronicles of the Kings, the church must gain an understanding of the times. *To speak the language of the lost, the Church must become cultural exegetes with "feet on the street."* Christians must engage communities with love, for without love, Christians will never earn the right to be heard. *Churches must create a culture of discipleship by delineating a pathway to spiritual maturity.* Pastors and teachers must resist a hermeneutic that engages the mind but does not transform the heart. Christian leaders must also make room for those with doubts, for doubts; when properly processed, can actually bring people closer to Jesus.

In the 1939 musical, *The Wizard of Oz*, Dorothy awakens in an unfamiliar place and famously says, "Toto, I've a feeling we're not in Kansas anymore." Perhaps

AWAKENING THE CHURCH IN NORTH AMERICA

that is a feeling all pastors and churches share in this 21st century. Though unfamiliar, it is a world filled with people that God loves and for whom He gave His Son.

Creating a culture of discipleship within and through local churches is not simple—often easier said than done. Drawing the strategy on a white board is too often far removed from doing the real work of discipleship. The work of discipleship requires action and the understanding that discipleship *is* work. For many churches in today's world this is a paradigm from an inward focus to outward transformation. It is a shift from a *"sit-and-watch church culture"* to a *"knowing, being, and doing"* church culture.

No Excuses

A new paradigm has shifted into place in recent years, moving believers from a "church mind-set" to a "Kingdom mind-set." This cultural shift has thrust the Church into a harvest field in North America that is beckoning for reapers. Understanding the urgency of the harvest is awakening the saints. The Church must rethink approaches to the harvest. Within a diverse population, opportunities for ministry and discipleship abound as never before.

Pastors Victor and Jamie Massey shared how their

PROACTIVE IN POST-CHRISTIAN CULTURE

previous congregation in the Atlanta, Georgia, area consisted of over forty nations, so they learned to be sensitive to the mixture of religious backgrounds that diversity can bring. The challenge for discipleship required recognizing and adapting to cultural barriers. The Masseys relied on the Holy Spirit to translate in ways that crumbled those barriers. There are absolutely no excuses for not reaching the harvest. John 4:35 admonishes believers to cast off any blinders that lead to procrastination. The Lord knows the exact plan for every person, regardless of whether they are inside the church building or not. Jesus loves them all, and so must all believers.

Currently, this same pastoral couple serves a church in a rural area of Alabama, where poverty and addiction plague the community. As a result of prayerful research, the Lord directed this church to purchase an old school and convert it into the City of Lights Dream Center of Walker County to address the issues in that declining community. Organizations and other churches have all joined hands to help reap this harvest. An awakening is occurring as the community comes alive again.

Working the harvest together, this couple found that the spiritual needs were great. People are thirsty to believe that God cares for them! They are hungry to experience His love. Christians must awaken and "lift up [their] eyes and look at the fields!" (John 4:35 NKJV). Pastors and church members don't always know what the lost need, but the Holy Spirit does. He provides strategic methods for reaping in the fields. The conditions are exactly right for this tremendous harvest to be gathered. When it comes to the harvest, churches cannot make excuses. They must see through the eyes of the Holy Spirit to find an abundant opportunity for harvest.

Culture Shifts, the Mission Does Not

The Great Commission is still real and relevant in the 21st century. This is still truth, in spite of societal shifts and changes. In this atmosphere, the Church has an obligation to be strategic and vigilant in its work to understand context and culture, develop relationships within the community, and perpetually make disciples who make disciples. Pastors, church leaders, and members must commit to becoming more proactive in this post-Christian culture in order to reach people before it is too late. This calling, commission, and task is hard work and requires commitment. However, the harvest is more than worth the effort!

Collaborative Team Members for "Proactive in Post-Christian Culture"

Sean O'Neal, Collaborative Coach
Administrative Bishop, Church of God,
California/Nevada Region

Jamie Massey
Copastor and Executive Director, Sumiton Church of
God, Sumiton, Alabama

B. Randall Parris
International Coordinator, Global Youth Leader,
Youth and Discipleship, Church of God International
Offices, Cleveland, Tennessee

Tony Stewart
Lead Pastor, City Life Church of God, Tampa, Florida

Mark L. Williams
Lead Pastor, North Cleveland Church of God,
Cleveland, Tennessee

5

COMMUNICATION THAT CONNECTS

*"How then shall they call on Him in whom they have not
believed? And how shall they believe in Him of whom they have
not heard? And how shall they hear without a preacher?"*
(Romans 10:14 NKJV).

Communication intelligence and relational skills are
vital to a spiritual awakening. Life-giving connections can
be made where a rapport exists between a speaker and a
listener. Since relevance and empathy are key to gaining
people's attention, ministers who are able to relate to
people's life experiences and values can be effective in
leading them to Christ.

Preaching and teaching are two of the most important
means of communication in ministry. However, there
are additional tools that support and enhance further
connection. Church leaders should consider a "by all
means" approach (see 1 Corinthians 9:22) and employ
the use of logos, religious symbols, appropriate signage,
church websites, and the wise use of social media.

The goal of sharing the gospel of Jesus is to impact souls for eternity. God's kingdom is perfectly holy; therefore, Christians should strive for honesty and authenticity in all communication about the Kingdom. Authenticity is highly esteemed in today's culture. Many people can spot a phony a mile away. If they even suspect that an inauthentic person is leading in ministry, that ministry is virtually doomed by common standards.

Modern ministers must make sure their methods do not hinder the spread of the Gospel to this generation. Like relevancy, much has been said recently about excellence in ministry. Christians are ambassadors of heaven and represent the very kingdom of God. Anything less than the very best in ministry is less than He deserves and requires. Three communication components—*authenticity*, *relevancy*, and *excellence*—deserve attention.

Authenticity in Communication

Dictionaries define *authentic* as "of undisputed origin; genuine." Synonyms include: *genuine, real, bona fide, true,* and *veritable. Authenticity* signifies whether or not someone is believable. Regardless of what is said or how it is said, if no one believes it, the effort to share the Gospel is essentially negated. Authenticity is a nonnegotiable for ministry today.

COMMUNICATION THAT CONNECTS

Because communication techniques evolve over time, aspects of modern communication deserve consideration. Scriptures are replete with examples of how communication tools changed, depending on the crowd being addressed. At times, Jesus preached from a boat; at other times, He sat on a hillside. He wrote in the sand and He told stories. He spoke gently to the children, but He harshly rebuked the Pharisees. While He changed His approach from time to time, Jesus did not adjust the heart of the message in an effort to please the crowds.

Pastor Jason Isaacs in Louisville, Kentucky, states, "Jesus knew who He was and what He was called to do. He came to minister to the sick (not the healthy) through teaching, healing, and ultimately the Cross. He did not adjust His ministry to the whims of culture or the demands of the crowds. He led and spoke authentically, and people are always attracted to authenticity." Even a controversial message is more welcomed when the speaker is genuine. Authenticity is crucial to the Gospel message being openly received and believed.

Authenticity also involves integrity. Actions must be congruent with words. If a preacher passionately preaches holiness, but his or her personal life indicates deception, integrity is lost. If church signage and websites promise one thing, but a personal visit reveals something quite different, credibility is forfeited. If social media touts an exceptional worship service, but those who attend the service have a different interpretation, trustworthiness is called into question. If preachers exaggerate while preaching, if sermon illustrations are historically or statistically inaccurate, if leaders plagiarize, or preach the sermons of others without proper credit, listeners will view them as inauthentic, hindering the Gospel message.

Communications specialist Chad Guyton does an excellent job of describing the value of story in today's communication. He shares that throughout Pentecostal history, storytelling has been central to experiencing God. Testimony services and fellowship gatherings bonded and encouraged congregations as people shared personal encounters with the Holy Spirit. Guyton explains that if current listeners can identify with the experience being shared in a story, much of the battle of believability and credibility is already won. The elements of trust and empathy are engaged when people relate to a story. In order to effectively reach people, Christ followers must again embrace and share the stories of God intersecting with their personal lives. Preaching and teaching must include stories.

Stories Create Believability and Authenticity

Online and social media communication on the part of ministries must be wrapped in a story. If people perceive that churches are simply selling a product, the effectiveness of that ministry is greatly hindered. Guyton says, "A church's online and social media presence shouldn't be used as a sales pitch to potential customers looking for a product. Instead, it must invite people to see themselves as a character in a story of God's faithfulness, opening the door for an encounter with the true Author of that story." If a church's or Christian's story is not believable, if listeners cannot identify with what is said and done, if the story seems fabricated or implausible, effectiveness will wane, and the crowds will diminish. Poor communication ultimately leads to not effectively reaching people.

Preaching and teaching has changed dramatically with the advent of the Internet search. Listeners can instantly search the Web for sources of information. Until just a few years ago, preachers were relatively safe from the "verification police" or any efforts to discredit their

AWAKENING THE CHURCH IN NORTH AMERICA

> **Within seconds of a particular claim made from the pulpit, savvy listeners can confirm the accuracy via their smart phone.**

preaching. This is no longer the case. Within seconds of a particular claim made from the pulpit, savvy listeners can confirm the accuracy via their smart phone. The lesson for church leaders is to do research ahead of time to be sure they know what they are talking about. It is not just cynics or skeptics trying to catch preachers in error that motivates these efforts. Today's generation is fact-driven, and they want to trust those who influence them. Rather than seeing the Internet as the enemy of preaching, ministers and pastors should embrace it as an invaluable tool that will increase effectiveness. It could be assumed that if a man or woman would mislead a crowd with statistics or historical data, they might

> **It is not just cynics or skeptics trying to catch preachers in error that motivates these efforts. Today's generation is fact-driven, and they want to trust those who influence them.**

also mislead the crowd about the Bible.

Authenticity matters! Christians must be real,

120

COMMUNICATION THAT CONNECTS

showing integrity in everything they do and say. Those who hear the Gospel message will discern the authenticity or inauthenticity of the ministry and the message, and will react accordingly.

Relevancy in Communication

Not only should today's minister and layperson focus on authenticity, but also on relevancy. Of course, the Bible is relevant and applicable to every generation. Its message never changes. But if the Church is not intentional about relevancy, she may make the mistake of unintentionally miscommunicating the Bible with language or methods that are no longer understood.

Veteran church attenders have witnessed the evolution of language. The frequent change in the use and meaning of words may leave the Church behind. It can be a mistake to try to use language that is popular in the culture without digging deep into definitions. But it can also be a mistake to refuse to change the language that has been used for many years. Great discretion must be utilized when considering the relevancy of ministry language. Avoiding "Christianese" (the language only understood by longstanding Christians) should be avoided when trying to reach a lost culture.

AWAKENING THE CHURCH IN NORTH AMERICA

Skilled ministry leaders must learn how to utilize modern language without compromising the depth of the Gospel message. Refusal to engage in ministry with modern language is not a sign of godliness; but could instead be a potential sign of stubbornness. Who stands to benefit if a minister or church goes to great lengths to use words that have lost their meaning and impact? The truth of God's love is simple enough for children to comprehend. The Gospel should never be presented in a way that is less than understandable. Relevancy is not the same as "watering down the Word" or "dumbing down the Scriptures." Since the beginning of time, language continues to evolve and develop. God's Word is alive and deserves a language that is also fully alive.

Effective communicators will not back away from the challenge of finding new ways of communicating ageless truth. This is precisely what Jesus did while He was on the earth. This is an important principle to ponder: Jesus ministered in such a way that people who didn't yet believe wanted to come and hear Him speak. The Church must follow in the ways of Christ. Today's generation deserves the opportunity to hear the Gospel presented in fresh new ways. God still utilizes willing vessels to communicate His Word so lives can be changed.

COMMUNICATION THAT CONNECTS

Though the Gospel message never changes, the words used to explain the Gospel remain fluid. However, the basic principles of communication are steady. When Jesus walked the earth, people who heard Him invited others to come hear Him. He had "the words of eternal life (John 6:68 NKJV). This principle is so simple it almost sounds inadequate, but it is not. Crowds came to hear Jesus because someone invited them to come. Some two thousand years later, not much has changed. If people hear about life-giving churches in a compelling and relevant way, the chances are good that they will come and see. But, how can people in the community come if they are never invited or compelled to come in relevant ways? Is it possible that believers have the life-giving message, but the presentation is so dead that no one is compelled to listen?

An often-contentious discussion in modern ministry centers on style. Human nature gravitates toward comfort. People are prone to find a comfort zone of communication, usually based on experiences, and they stick with that style. Ministry communication is not exempt from this same phenomenon. It is easy to embrace what is familiar and comfortable. However,

123

AWAKENING THE CHURCH IN NORTH AMERICA

not everyone was raised within the church. Is it possible that the style of church one generation grew up in is fundamentally ineffective in reaching another listener or the next generation of listeners?

The Church can't afford to make the mistake of limiting the power of the Gospel because of a refusal to explore the possibility of improving communication effectiveness. The message of the Gospel is holy, but the methods of communicating the Gospel are not. While the mission of the Church is to reach the lost, a few churches have adopted the counterfeit mission of fighting to maintain adherence to a comfortable, familiar, almost obsolete style of ministry or preferred choice of communication.

There is certainly nothing wrong with preferring a particular preaching or teaching style, but it is small thinking to assume that one style is the only correct style. As has been stated, even Jesus adjusted His approach, based on His listeners. A common misconception in ministry is that a message has to be intense, loud, or serious in order to be spiritual, but Jesus didn't embody that. He told stories about farms and sat in boats on the lake. He sat at kitchen tables, asked questions, and helped people believe they were better than their worst mistakes.

COMMUNICATION THAT CONNECTS

Inspiration and encouragement are always compelling. The church's challenge is to take ancient truth and communicate it in modern, relevant, and effective ways. If successful in doing so, this generation, as well as those to come, will respond with open hearts and minds to God's Word.

Please do not dismiss better communication as an effort to simply be "cool." The ultimate goal is not to be perceived as modern or trendy, but to present the Gospel in clear and understandable ways. Marty Baker emphasizes this at Stevens Creek, the church he and his wife, Patty, planted more than thirty years ago and still lead today. He often says, "Clear is better than cool! We must work to be relevant and focus on being clear with the message of the Gospel. The reason we do these things is so that people in our community will come to hear a clear presentation of the Gospel and respond accordingly." If the message is cool but not clear, the goal was completely missed.

The Church faces the challenge of addressing a distracted audience with an ageless message. Clarity is a must. This chaotic, digital, social-media-driven world gives only a few precious seconds to capture someone's attention,

AWAKENING THE CHURCH IN NORTH AMERICA

and if God's Word is not clearly communicated, it may have eternal consequences for someone who needed the good news. This approach requires great discipline and determination on the part of modern ministry communicators. Pastors must be lifelong learners. Christians must be students of the Word as well as of culture. Followers of Christ must engage others, perhaps those younger than they are, by developing better communication models. Church members and leaders must be wise in the Spirit as well as in social contexts. Determine today to declare the Word of God with clarity, relevance, and effectiveness. Otherwise, this generation could be lost, and Christians will bear the brunt of the responsibility.

Technology Has Changed Everything

In 2007, the concept of carrying the Internet in a trouser pocket was introduced when Steve Jobs (founder and CEO of Apple, Inc.) walked on a stage and unveiled the first iPhone. Since then, daily life has evolved from being enhanced by technology to having all kinds of technology woven into the fabric of personal communication. People experience, document, and share life events in real time via social media through text, images, and video.

These advancements in technology have not only impacted personal interactions but also changed the way the average person receives news, experiences entertainment, and completes common daily tasks like shopping and commuting. Tasks that once required a phone call or being physically present are now completed with a few taps on one's mobile device.

It is imperative that every local church pastor and leader be in tune and in sync with the people in the pews. There is sometimes a disconnect between the knowledge within the minds of the church constituents and that of the pastor. Many parishioners are immersed and informed by technology—it influences the way they think, communicate, and interact on a daily basis. However, it is often the church leaders and/or pastor who are hindered by their fears of irrelevancy. Though unintended, pastors sometimes allow their inadequacies to slow church growth and progress. It is impossible to effectively fight an enemy without knowing and understanding the enemy's weapons of choice. Church

> **Church leaders and pastors must restock their arsenal using technology and social media to fight successfully.**

leaders and pastors must restock their arsenal using technology and social media to fight successfully.

When social media in the form of websites like Twitter and Facebook arrived on the scene, many immediately saw it as a way to maintain connections with friends and family, lessening the feeling of disconnect that distance and separation create. It was an amazing new way to experience events from someone else's perspective. In those early days, before content feeds became filled with pictures of food, babies, memes, and personal-life moments that should probably remain "personal," checking Twitter was more about catching up on news and the daily happenings of friends and family. Since those early days, social networks have evolved into a primary source of information, communication, and news.

Just Answer the Question

It would be foolish to assume the Church is somehow immune or exempt from these technological advancements. If anything, current content and media consumption trends represent the opportunity for a paradigm shift in the way the local church approaches its worship experience and missional obligations. Decoding the formula to success in this new arena of media and technology

COMMUNICATION THAT CONNECTS

is, at the least, complex. Yet, at the same time, utilizing technology represents a unique path to directly connect with people in ways that extend beyond the setting of a worship service.

The question facing every pastor and church leader is, "Can our church be relevant and relational in this Internet-driven culture?" The simple answer is, a local church will struggle to survive in the future if every effort is not made to understand and interact through social media and Internet-driven experiences. Learning how to effectively utilize these new platforms requires a willingness for pastors and church members to incorporate new methods of communication and interaction while maintaining the foundations and principles by which the church is established.

The good news is, though the social/Internet platform represents a massive strategic shift from the classical approach to local church ministry, the powerful story of the Gospel message remains the same and continues to deliver the same life-changing impact as always. It is perhaps here that media poses the greatest opportunity for Pentecostals regarding ministry and the Great Commission. Social media provides a forum to bring Christian testimony into an instantaneous, global conversation. Platforms like Facebook, Instagram, Twitter, and others provide opportunities for Gospel witness on an unprecedented scale.

If Jesus was anything, He was a storyteller. Scripture indicates Jesus was a carpenter, but does not record His wood-carving exploits. What the Bible does reveal repeatedly are the stories He told, using that age-old process to communicate complicated concepts in relatively simple ways. The Bible itself is a story. Technology and social media provide the Church with an astonishing variety of opportunities to share stories of what God has done in our Christian communities and in our own lives.

Use Technology for Spreading the Gospel; Just Use It Wisely!

In terms of an overarching vision of how the ministry and the Great Commission might be advanced through media, some of the greatest potential lies not only in the capacity for Christians to tell their stories to the world, but also in the opportunity for the world to tell its stories to the Church. You didn't misread that. One of the greatest resources the Church now has to accomplish

COMMUNICATION THAT CONNECTS

God's work is the new capability of the Church to hear and see stories from the world in a different way. In many cases, the Christian's capacity to embrace the fullness of the mission has been stunted by the disconnection from profound global stories of pain, suffering, and injustice. The grasp of the Church's mission will be limited at best if she does not have a clear vision of the world's deep need as a backdrop.

People are utilizing social media and technology as tools to pursue ministry and fulfillment of the Great Commission in diverse forms and contexts. There is a new, common thread showing up in successful churches— leaders who demonstrate remarkable intentionality in how they use media. Some church leaders are reflective, thoughtful, and even reverent about how they use these alternately wonderful and dangerous new tools. If there is any danger in appropriating these tools in a Pentecostal context, it is that we might attempt to use these new methods without exercising sensible caution.

When we have such powerful tools at our disposal, making it possible for us to broadcast our every thought and whim to the world with such ease, the key to using media for the church's mission may lie as much in our *restraint* as in our *creativity*. Having personal opinions is not inherently a bad thing. Sharing them in a cavalier manner, on the other hand, can be devastating when attempting to use media to help make disciples. It's not about shying away when one feels God has given them something bold to say, but about having a proper sense of weight to one's calling and to one's words.

God has provided many new tools to use to continue our mission of making disciples of all the nations. Jonathan Martin, pastor of The Table church in Oklahoma City, warns, use social media but for the sake of Christ and His kingdom—use it well, use it wisely, use it cautiously. The urgency of the task and the power of these tools are far too great for anything less. In the context of this swirling maze of testimonies, how peculiar and how wonderful it is to share or hear a story of someone being saved, sanctified, and filled with the Holy Spirit!

Engage People Personally

The Church must take advantage of technology, but must also engage with people personally. In times past, church leaders enjoyed more physical access to church members. Social life in many towns centered on the church. Before the advent of electricity and media entertainment, there wasn't much competition for people's attention. Obviously, this is no longer the case. It seems the lives of most people are increasingly busy with no end in sight. Rather than one or two opportunities (Sunday services), it is time to grab hold of other opportunities to connect with people.

Pastor Eli Bonilla of Abundant Life Church in San Antonio, Texas, believes the Gospel is best communicated when it is shared exponentially. Rather than providing only one or two opportunities a week to preach the Gospel (traditional worship services), he strives to release members into hundreds of weekly meetings in homes, cafés, community centers, and so on, so that the church engages people with the Gospel message where they are. While some churches still conduct worship services on Sunday morning and Sunday evening, along with midweek Bible study, weekly prayer meetings, and revivals, fewer and fewer churches find this schedule possible.

Jesus met people where they were and led them to where they needed to be. In the modern world, if people are not coming to church services, perhaps the church should take the services to them. Jesus knew His most effective ministry was done through investing Himself into His inner circle of close followers; that's why He spent 73 percent of His time in the Gospels with just twelve disciples. Rather than seeing declining attendance at church services as a negative, perhaps ministering one-on-one and in smaller groups is part of the solution. Perhaps more disciples would be made if the original method as detailed in the Gospels was employed.

While not every church can or should provide online access to their services, many should. Live streaming, radio, television broadcasts, and podcasts are just a few of the ways modern churches can reach outside their four walls. The New Testament model of church was not confined to a church building. The Book of Acts clearly details ministry in the community (among the people), in everyday life situations. A Biblically based model of outreach releases ministry outside the confines of a building.

One of the challenges Spirit-filled churches encounter today is how the movement of the Spirit is experienced in less traditional ministry settings. Pastors are adept at the operation of the Spirit in corporate gatherings, but what does that look like in public places? How does a pastor or leader safeguard the Biblical integrity of prophecy, speaking in tongues and interpretation and words of

COMMUNICATION THAT CONNECTS

wisdom or words of knowledge, if the church is meeting in nontraditional settings? Holy Spirit empowerment never grows old or becomes outdated. Limiting the power of the Spirit because of a refusal to grow with the Spirit limits what God can do!

Successful pastors like Eli Bonilla focus on a relevant message that prevents the church from becoming irrelevant and disconnected from culture. He believes Wesleyan roots and Pentecostal presentation are what set Pentecostals apart from other ministries and, therefore, works to an advantage. Instead of disconnecting from the community because of heritage, believers should engage the power of the Spirit so that the message remains relevant, powerful, and life-changing for the people

> **The always-relevant work of the Holy Spirit is able to draw North America to God!**

in the congregation and community. God designed the Church to thrive in every generation. The always-relevant work of the Holy Spirit is able to draw North America to God!

Excellence Matters, but "Pobody Is Nerfect"

Everything done in the name of the Lord should be

done with excellence. Excellence is not to be confused with perfection. No one is capable of achieving perfection on this earth, but everyone is required by God to offer Him their very best. Excellence should be the standard for all ministry communication. Whether it involves social media, sermons, lessons, hospitality, websites, signage—everything that communicates the message should be presented at the highest standard.

What do misspelled words in song lyrics communicate? If the church bulletin is boring, does it matter? If a church sign is faded, the paint is peeling and the words are difficult to read, who cares? People who don't attend that church care! Of course, they are not part of the church family, so are the signs, or song lyrics, or church bulletins any of their business? Yes, it is their business, and any church leaders who do not recognize this may already be detached from their mission.

Not All Communication is Verbal or Written

Misspelled words communicate lack of effort. Greeters who are so busy talking among themselves that they ignore guests send a strong message of exclusion, even if unintentional. A dilapidated sign says, "What's the difference, anyway?" Tall grass, peeling paint, dirty restrooms, and smelly church basements communicate loud and clear that ministry and excellence are not priorities. These things tell the world that the church cannot be troubled to expend time and energy to make things nice. Remember, clean does not mean expensive. It is true that many churches cannot afford to provide all of the modern conveniences for their members. But it costs very little to provide a clean restroom.

Some smaller churches lack the space and resources to provide a state-of-the-art facility for babies. No one can expect a small church to have facilities like a megachurch. But few parents of infants are comfortable leaving their children in a nursery that includes spider webs, unemptied diaper pails, dingy cribs, or exposed electrical outlets. Churches that do not focus on providing an excellent nursery communicate many things to young parents like, "Your children are not very important to us." Heartbreaking, isn't it? It's true that some potential attenders demand perfection and hold the church to an impossibly high standard. But the babies (and the Lord) still deserve the very best.

That's a Wrap!

A few Pentecostals may contend that quality does

AWAKENING THE CHURCH IN NORTH AMERICA

not matter; anointing is all that matters. It is true, after all, that a person does not need to be an expert to be effective. Does this emphasis on excellence sound carnal? Excellence is an achievable standard. Striving for excellence in communication is a sacrificial offering to God. A ministry that emphasizes increasing quality will reach more people for Christ. God gave His very best in Jesus Christ; followers of Christ must refuse to offer the Lord anything but their absolute best.

The Gospel message is the most important message ever shared. Communicating an excellent message with excellent methods honors God, and more people will be compelled to follow Christ. If by improving speaking and writing, being intentionally authentic, and striving for excellence the church can reignite North America to Christ, by all means, the church should do so!

COMMUNICATION THAT CONNECTS

Collaborative Team Members for "Communication That Connects"

Rick Whitter, Collaborative Coach
Administrative Bishop, Church of God, State of Illinois

Marty Baker
Lead Pastor, Stevens Creek Church of God,
Augusta, Georgia

Eliezer Bonilla
Pastor, Vida Abundante Church of God,
San Antonio, Texas

Chad Guyton
Media Professional, Communications, Church of God
International Offices, Cleveland, Tennessee

Jason Isaacs
Senior Pastor, Hope City Church, Shepherdsville,
Kentucky

Rob Maggard
Coordinator of Branding and Marketing,
Communications, Church of God International Offices,
Cleveland, Tennessee

6

COSIDERING YESTERDAY
CONCEIVING TOMORROW

*"Brethren, I do not count myself to have apprehended; but one
thing I do, forgetting those things which are behind and reaching
forward to those things which are ahead, I press toward the goal
for the prize of the upward call of God in Christ Jesus"*
(Philippians 3:13-14 NKJV).

The apostle Paul was consumed with a calling to
know Christ and make Him known! He never felt that he
was finished, or his work completed. He said, "One thing
I do: Forgetting what is behind and straining toward
what is ahead, I press on toward the goal" (Phil. 3:13-14
NIV). He was totally dedicated to personal intimacy with
Christ, preaching the Gospel, equipping believers, and
organizing churches.

The first-generation Christians followed suit—going
everywhere preaching the Gospel to every person and
making disciples. A car may be recalled to the dealership,
but God has not recalled the Church. There has never

been a "stop work" order in the Church. We have not yet heard the Spirit say to the Church, "It is finished." Children continue to be born, immigrants come to America, and the unchurched live in our communities. Therefore, we are compelled to grow, preach, baptize, equip, and organize more churches.

Many Christians have, intentionally or unintentionally, intellectually rationalized many prophecies and mysteries in the Bible. By doing so, some of the importance and wonder of those scriptural prototypes are forgotten or lost. Believers may have an intellectual understanding of the Great Commission, yet their actions of reaching the lost are minimal. Our knowledge needs our initiative and God's wisdom to go forward in faith. It is not enough to know something; knowledge must lead to action!

A New Church Planting Movement

Today almost everyone in North America has accessibility to tools and resources on church planting, sermon development, and building church structures at their fingertips. When someone feels the "spiritual nudge" to plant a church, in time, it often becomes a burning desire that must be answered. When God calls someone to plant a church, He is also ready to equip them for the

CONSIDERING YESTERDAY CONCEIVING TOMORROW

job. Through prayer, the Holy Spirit can lead church planters to the resources they need. People, finances, and knowledge can all come to those who pray and obey. God's favor often follows obedience to His call.

As a young man with a call, James Izzard had a spiritual zeal that was somewhat unchecked and unencumbered, so he simply launched into a public preaching ministry. While schools and seminaries have existed for centuries, they were not feasible options for James. By utilizing Bible studies and lively fellowships, Pastor Izzard's various ministry efforts converged to create an environment where God moved in powerful and expeditious ways. Spiritual awakening infuses a sense of newness and freshness into the body of Christ and plays a significant role ushering in church planting.

Scripture demonstrates that some of the most significant moments in Christendom came through the work of unassuming servants who simply responded to "spiritual nudges" from the Lord. In North America, a new church-planting movement has begun with men and women approaching ministry by asking themselves, "Why not me?" James Izzard took that approach, and God blessed his prayerful obedience.

143

The Race of a Lifetime

Life is more like a marathon, not a sprint. As a runner prepares for a race, he or she looks at the course set before them. The course is predetermined, and the runners cannot change it. Unfortunately, life does not give all the participants a life-course map. It would be beneficial if everyone knew where the hills and flats of life were, but no such map exists. A long-distance runner must accept whatever comes his or her way. The one thing a runner knows for sure is that the course will not stay the same.

Pastor Chris Gilbert's church-planting experience has certainly had some unexpected hills and curves for him to navigate. When his journey started, Chris Gilbert was minding his own business doing student ministry at a large church and enjoying life. He and his family were in a season of God's favor and blessing. They lived in a great house, had a wonderful church family, and no plans for doing anything different in the near future. However, God began stirring something in Chris's heart. It couldn't be that God was asking him to give up everything he had worked so hard to achieve, could it? Surely, God didn't want him to sell his house with the man cave, move his six-year-old daughter from her friends, and leave their almost-

CONSIDERING YESTERDAY CONCEIVING TOMORROW

perfect situation? But that is exactly what God wanted. God was calling Chris and his family to plant a church. Chris confesses that he always made fun of his friends who chose to plant churches. "Why would you want to do that?" he would ask. As it turns out, God had an even better season in store for Pastor Gilbert and his family.

Chris planted Vertical Church near Indianapolis after a church-planting network (ARC) graciously picked them up three weeks before the first Sunday. The fledgling church met for four and one-half years in a hotel, doing baptisms in the hotel pool and meetings in less-than-desirable conference rooms. But God blessed them and the church actually grew, to the surprise of many people. After nearly five years in a mediocre hotel, God opened the door to lease an old, run-down church building. Through this process, Chris learned to be faithful with what he had. Because he was faithful in stewardship during that season, God opened the next door. The church purchased that building, put a large amount of work into it, and they now have a church home of which to truly be proud.

Vertical Church went from one service to three services every Sunday, and they are now in the process of planting another campus, all to the glory of God. Pastor Chris is convinced of the wonderful faithfulness of God. He said, "The Lord has provided for and blessed my family more than words can say. What I thought was a huge risk ended up being the journey of a lifetime. He is ready to do the same in your life. Will you say yes?"

Christians need to ask themselves if they are ready to go another mile or if they will just pull over and wait for the "glory bus" to pick them up and take them to heaven. That may seem harsh, but so many others have sacrificed, pushed forward, and worked continuously to accomplish the work of the Lord. It's how the Church has gotten this far. Church planting is the key to fulfilling the Great Commission. It could very well be this generation that finishes the Great Commission—the finish line is in sight!

The Calling of a Church Planter

All church planters have a different story of how they were called; no two are exactly alike. Church planting goes beyond ministry. It requires a complete buy-in from everyone, not just the pastor. There are many costs to consider when planting a church, including financial. For the pastor, church planting requires a huge commitment of personal time, emotional investment, and strong

CONSIDERING YESTERDAY CONCEIVING TOMORROW

mental capacity. When the call to plant a church is placed on someone, it is no small thing. At first, most feel it is an almost impossible thing. The Lord has a plan He wants to share with every church planter He calls. It is so important to remember this is His plan, His timing, and that He is the provider.

Brent Stephens was a youth pastor in South Georgia and had set an aggressive deadline for the opening of a new student center. He found himself hanging sheetrock all alone at 4:00 a.m. *What is this all for?* was the question he kept asking the Lord. After repeating the question several times, he received his answer. It was not a clear and audible voice—it was a still, small voice in Brent's spirit. *I'm preparing you to plant a church.* At the time, Brent had never thought of church planting and had no context for what a church plant even was. He simply tucked it away into the back of his mind.

Sometimes, God's love is so great that He will not let His children miss a blessing. He pursues His children, longing for someone to step out into the unknown in faith. Trusting in the sovereignty of God and His promises means obedient believers must surrender themselves. Many times, a church planter must embrace Jesus' statement in Luke 22:42: "Nevertheless not My will, but Yours, be done" (NKJV).

This calling caused Brent to quit his job without knowing where he and his wife, Sarah, were going, or how the church plant was going to work. Their calling moved them to Acworth, Georgia, where they didn't know anyone, and compelled Brent to teach school while they built their core group in the evenings. This calling kept them going when donor checks did not come from people who said they would send them. It also kept them committed when they were discouraged and wanted to quit. They were unwavering in answering the call.

Questions for Every Church Planter to Answer

> **There is no doubt, a church planter needs to feel a special call of God on his or her life to plant a church.**

There is no doubt, a church planter needs to feel a special call of God on his or her life to plant a church. Here are a few questions to ask to determine if church planting is truly God's will:

1. *What educational, life experience, or ministerial practice does one have that might help qualify them to plant a church?* Many people think God knocked Saul

CONSIDERING YESTERDAY CONCEIVING TOMORROW

off his horse and he was the famous apostle Paul the very next day. The reality is, God sent Paul into the wilderness for three years, and *then* had the Church send him out (Galatians 1:17-18; Acts 13:1-3).

2. *Do the spouse and children of the church planter also feel the calling of God on the entire family to plant a church?* Family is the first priority and highest calling of any committed minister. This is why those who lead the Church must prove themselves by first managing their own families (1 Timothy 3:4). A church planter cannot do this assignment alone. Every church planter needs their family fully engaged and completely on board.

3. *Is there any other kind of ministry a potential church planter could do and feel fulfilled?* Each believer has different gifts according to the purpose of the Holy Spirit (see 1 Corinthians 12:4-11; Ephesians 4:11-12). If teaching is a primary gifting, that person may be well-suited and easily fulfilled by teaching in an existing church setting. To plant a church, a strong apostolic pull of the one who is called and sent to a specific place is absolutely.

Infamous Words of a Church Planter

Anthony Braswell is another successful church planter. He is also director of church planting for the Acts 2 Network. He remembers saying when he was younger, "I would never plant a church!" His wife, Mary Ann, also said she would never marry a pastor; yet, here they are.

It's interesting how personal plans are often so much different than what God has planned. While Anthony was serving as a state youth and discipleship director, a discerning pastor friend asked him, "If a minister is 'living the dream,' why are they often so miserable?" It was obvious to Anthony that something else was on his heart. What his friend did discern was a battle Anthony was fighting internally about God's ultimate plan for his family and ministry. Anthony's friend asked him, "If you could do anything you wanted for two years and not worry about how you would be paid to do it, what would you do?" For the first time in his life, Anthony confessed out loud, "I would plant a church in Raleigh, North Carolina!"

When Anthony and Mary Ann moved to Raleigh, the Holy Spirit spoke words over his life that would forever change him. The Lord said, *I'm not calling you to raise up a group of people you can pastor. I'm calling you to raise*

CONSIDERING YESTERDAY CONCEIVING TOMORROW

up a group of people who will pastor your city! What powerful words! If we truly believe all souls matter to God, we must do whatever it takes to reach the unsaved. Followers of Jesus must become *comfortable* with being *uncomfortable.* Life with people is extremely

> **The Lord said,** *I'm not calling you to raise up a group of people you can pastor. I'm calling you to raise up a group of people who will pastor your city!*

messy, but Jesus encourages His followers to spend time and extend love to those who are hurting, broken, sick, disgraced, or just messed up.

Jesus provided the greatest example. When He saw the crowds, the Bible says He had "compassion" (see Matthew 9:36; Mark 6:34). Jesus didn't make it easy for Himself by avoiding people's troubles; He waded in and helped out. Here are a few important concepts for every church planter to consider:

- *Teamwork makes the dream work.* A believer's highest calling is to equip *others* to do the work of ministry. Invest in their spiritual lives, their families, and their leadership development. Be the *example* of the rule, not the *exception.*
- *Reach their family without sacrificing yours.* As much as Anthony loved the people in his city, he decided not to reach their families at the expense of his own. He intentionally chose not

151

to sacrifice the health of his marriage and family in an effort to grow the church. Church planters don't have to worry; Jesus loves His Church more than they do! Church planters must love their family and be present in every moment.

- *Vision is awesome, but without a plan, it is only a daydream.* Church planters are typically *dreamers*. Dreams don't change the world, but the actions put behind them do. When church planters don't have a plan, they end up spinning their wheels for years, completely frustrated! These ministers must surround themselves with people who will help them develop an action plan to actually accomplish the things in their hearts.

Preaching Is Not Optional

A great deal of planning and preparation go into planting a church. Financing, logistics, volunteer training, and countless other tasks must be discussed and decided before the church launch date. It is not enough to assemble a group of people and start a new church. A Biblical church plant must also successfully accomplish the Great Commission (see Matthew 28:19-20). A crucial element to consider is how God's Word will be delivered. The Bible is the foundation of everything Christians do. Hebrews 11:6 states, "But without faith it is impossible to please Him, for he who comes to God must believe that He is, and that He is a rewarder of those who diligently

CONSIDERING YESTERDAY CONCEIVING TOMORROW

seek Him" (NKJV). The natural progression of this is found in Romans 10:17, "So then faith comes by hearing, and hearing by the Word of God" (NKJV). If a healthy, effective, life-giving church is to be established, it will primarily be through the preached Word of God.

Pastor Brent Stephens conveys some keen insights and personal observations on current pulpit ministry. Pulpit ministry has changed drastically in the last twenty-five years. Denominations and pastors have been highly influenced by movements dealing with church growth, positive thinking, prosperity, seeker-sensitivity, leadership, and postmodern emergent trends. Stephens believes while all these developments contain nuggets of wisdom, the cumulative result of this religious smorgasbord of consumeristic appeal is that it's hard to find a church that truly opens the Bible anymore! Building real Christian men and women who are faithfully living for Jesus in this world necessitates "preaching the Word" (see 2 Timothy 4:1-5; Romans 10:14).

One of the best things that happened in the history of this young church was when he made the decision to preach through books of the Bible. He was scared out of his mind! It seemed so boring and irrelevant to

153

AWAKENING THE CHURCH IN NORTH AMERICA

go chapter-by-chapter, verse-by-verse every Sunday. However, God had made the conviction clear on Brent's conscience. His own opinions, while cute, were not very helpful. If Brent really wanted to help people, then he must give them words he knew to be true in all situations, in all places, at all times; the only words that accomplish that are the words of God (2 Timothy 3:16). The reality of that decision was that the church lost some people; it didn't grow as fast as other churches that have thousands of people gather in just a few years.

However, the church saw growth—good, steady, healthy growth over the past decade. They started with seven young adults in his living room, and are now celebrating several hundred who come to one of the three weekend services. To Brent's great surprise, God's Word has never been irrelevant at any point. In fact, it continues to speak to the hearts of their current culture week after week.

The Gospel, which is found in the stories of the Old Testament and on every page of the New Testament, is the only force powerful enough to change the hard hearts of men and women. Speaking of sin and repentance, or judgment and hell, is not a very "positive" message, and

CONSIDERING YESTERDAY CONCEIVING TOMORROW

these things may often offend people. What is painfully ironic is, God says in His Word that people *will* be offended by this (see Matthew 10:22; 1 Corinthians 1:18; 1 Peter 2:7-8). If there has ever been a time to return to Scripture, it is now! Ministers must boldly preach God's Word. When His Word is preached,

> **If there has ever been a time to return to Scripture, it is now!**

people realize they are sinners in need of a Savior, and many will repent. They will turn to Jesus and grow in the power of His Spirit. When they hear God's Word, they will love His Church and joyfully serve and give.

It Is Not Easy, but It Is Worth It

Planting a church is never easy. In North America, this is accomplished by those who answer the call, setting aside personal agendas and following the leading and instruction of the Holy Spirit. It is by God's design that the Church will regain its power and become a mighty army again, with faithful men and women of the Cross who march into unfamiliar territories, set up camp, and acquire what God has promised in His Word.

God's plan is always so much better than our own plans. Be open to the imagination and God-sized cre-

AWAKENING THE CHURCH IN NORTH AMERICA

ativity given to us to share His message in a way that lives are forever changed. Step out in faith and learn that trusting God is much more than just preaching about it. Be encouraged to pursue the dreams and passions God has placed in your heart.

CONSIDERING YESTERDAY CONCEIVING TOMORROW

Collaborative Team Members for
"Pray and Obey"

D. J. Portell, Collaborative Coach
Certified Church Consultant, USA Missions, Church of
God International Offices, Cleveland, Tennessee

Chris Gilbert
Lead Pastor, Vertical Church, Plainfield, Indiana

James Izzard Jr.
Lead Pastor, Life Builders Church of God,
District Heights, Maryland

Brent Stephens
Pastor, Four Points Church, Acworth, Georgia

7

REACHING WHEREVER YOU ARE

"And he called his ten servants, and delivered them ten pounds, and said unto them, 'Occupy till I come'"
(Luke 19:13 KJV).

In 1568, Robert Hunt stood in a makeshift church, under an old awning made from a torn ship sail at the Jamestown settlement. It was a bold act of faith to be the foundation stone in establishing the first Protestant church in the New World. It is highly probable in this uncharted territory of wilderness, danger, fear, and overwhelming circumstances, that he may have lamented to God: "*Here?* God, You sent me *here?*"

God doesn't always send pastors and other Christ-followers to the easiest or most convenient places. In fact, He sends many of His people to unusual and remote places—places which at first may seem like assignments with "less honor," seemingly insignificant places when aligned against the mosaic of a greater world of possibilities. However,

AWAKENING THE CHURCH IN NORTH AMERICA

He also sends His people to massive urban sprawls where city limits, ethnic diversities, and populations can be an intimidating, daunting task. Cosmopolitan cities such as Los Angeles, New York, Miami, or Dallas are important places for the cultural captivation of the Gospel. Small towns and rural routes, dotted with "mom-and-pop" stores and Walmarts—places where everybody knows everybody—are also seen through the eyes of God with great value.

Cities and town squares, rural routes, and "mountain hollers" are all valuable to the mission of God. He sends His workers where people are—no matter where they live. Why? Because He loves people everywhere. Therefore, it does not matter where someone is, He wants them to help advance the kingdom of God. Not one urban city or small-town courthouse square is too big or too small for God's love to permeate its culture. Wherever you are, it may be easy to feel overwhelmed at the size of Babylon or the unimportance of Bethlehem; but be assured, God intends for every Christian and minister to flourish because He placed them there to bloom.

No skyscraper can inhibit potential, no rural community can resist change, and no unpaved road can hide one

REACHING WHEREVER YOU ARE

from the power of God's blessings. No matter where you are, ten simple principles can aid the destruction of hell's impact on an assigned place of ministry and firmly establish His kingdom presence in each city, town, or dirt road.

1. Re-Vision Is Possible, No Matter Where You Are

Dr. Bryan Cutshall knows what it is to dream a big dream, no matter where he found himself. He went to a small church on the outskirts of St. Louis, Missouri, as a young man. What he started with didn't look like much to the outside world. He had a building, and a few faithful saints who dared to dream with him. What would Dr. Cutshall advise? He says:

An old truism in American culture says, "What you see is what you get"—a haunting truth that can be ignored at some risk of personal peril. Many Christians live superficially and cannot attain depth past what is visible on the surface. You can never create what you cannot envision; you can never become what you cannot see; and you can never design a future you cannot perceive. True vision occurs when faith shows you what is beyond the surface, and "visioneering" is the strategic execution of that vision. Just as God took nothing and created something, Abraham walked by faith through nothing and saw a kingdom. In that same way, God continues to ask us: "What do you see?"

161

AWAKENING THE CHURCH IN NORTH AMERICA

Dr. Cutshall asks a very important question, "What do you see?" What can *you* see? Can you see what others cannot? Can you re-vision an amazing future?

Re-visioning a place into what God intends is required, no matter where you are located. Some may have assumed the leadership helm of a past, great, victorious church—a church filled with stories from the glory days. Such a church may even be a historical marker within a denomination; thus, defining its early moments as it became a movement. No matter the location, several goals must be met to re-vision the future. • *The mandate to "Wake up" is a fitting one, as awakening is the first step in actualizing a vision.* Early risers often awake excited and energized. The quiet, uninterrupted morning hours are their most creative. The morning is when Bryan Cutshall prays, writes, creates, plans, exercises, and dreams. Unless pastors and churches in North America wake up, pray, create, and strategize on a large scale, they will miss one of the greatest harvests ever assigned to the church—the last-days harvest. Ministries don't need a *revision* (a revised edition of the same thing), they need to *re-vision*. God's people must answer the Spirit's call to the Church in these last days.• *Rethink outreach ministry and get back into the communities.* Learn the difference between

REACHING WHEREVER YOU ARE

evangelism ministry and outreach ministry. *Evangelism* encompasses ministries like nursing-home visitation and jail ministry. *Outreach* is wrapping arms around the community with things like resources, service days, love weeks, and community events.

• *Learn the difference between "home culture" and "guest culture" in the local church.* In many churches, the home culture is so treasured that members and leaders are blind to the lack of guest culture, including things like good signage. It is too difficult in many churches to engage and disciple new converts, and equally as difficult to assimilate new families into the culture of the church. There is a difference between spirituality and "churchiness," and the latter can drive away the lost.

• *Bridge the gap between the generations and dismiss the distracting notions of "old school" and "new school."* Prioritize mentoring and family, and be willing to compromise by blending music styles and cultural traditions. Those who don't will lose one generation to satisfy another and will not sustain the church long-term.

• *Rekindle the culture of invitation.* Salvation begins with an invitation. Unless ministers can motivate their congregations to daily invite others as part of their Christian

AWAKENING THE CHURCH IN NORTH AMERICA

DNA, those churches will never influence their communities for Christ.

• *Expand the worldview.* The North American version of the Gospel does not translate around the world. Churches must reboot the New Testament principles of Church and community. Believers must see what God is doing everywhere and lay aside the Americanized version of Christianity. The best way to do this is to take leaders and staff on mission trips—the enemy of ignorance is travel.

• *Networking is the only way to broaden the reach and resource of the Great Commission.* Teams must carefully align with global strategies and organizations that are bringing real change and impact to the world.

Another program or remodel in churches is not needed. Some churches have modernized to the point of secularization. It is impossible to change the world with a superficial, secularized church. Remodeling and reprogramming only cater to well-fed Americans with these ideas. Re-visioning is about returning to the original plan of the New Testament Church, which is the hope and future of North America and the world.

2. Ethnic Diversity Can Be Established, No Matter Where You Are

The world is changing. The multicultural makeup of even the smallest towns is now merging into a beautiful tapestry of ethnic diversity. The Pew Research Center says by 2060, American culture will become considerably more diverse. In fact, since 1965, America has welcomed more than forty million immigrants to its shores. Of these forty million, half were Hispanic, and nearly one-third were of Asian descent. What does the Bible say about this multicultural world in which we are now living? "After these things I looked, and behold, a great multitude which no one could number, of all nations, tribes, peoples, and tongues, standing before the throne and before the Lamb, clothed with white robes, with palm branches in their hands" (Revelation 7:9 NKJV).

Such ethnicity will be the fabric for a multicultural heaven, which leads to some important questions:

- Does the racial makeup of your church reflect God's vision of the Kingdom?
- Does the cultural makeup of your church indicate that a broad spectrum of your community finds your church's Gospel witness to be compelling?

AWAKENING THE CHURCH IN NORTH AMERICA

- Does the ethnic makeup of your church reflect that you are leading the broader culture, or simply following a homogeneous crowd?

These are important questions, since no monoethnic church can be found in the New Testament. Diversity is no longer limited to the urban areas of America. Today, ethnic beauty has found its way into the most remote places.

Ethnic diversity can be achieved no matter the locale. Kyle Hinson has accomplished this in his Reading, Pennsylvania community. He says:

> As I sit on the front row and look on the church stage and see my African-American worship leader, I am grateful for our anointed praise. As I listen to a verse of worship in Spanish, I am reminded that such a language is cherished by at least 40 percent of our congregation. Even my executive pastor, Ibrahim Bangura, who was born a Muslim in Sierra Leone with his caucasian wife, greeting at the door of our church, remind me of the great importance of reaching the nations of this world, no matter where we are.

Ethnic diversity in the American church is not a sociology experiment. Christians are all called to become the people of God as a prophetic countercultural

REACHING WHEREVER YOU ARE

movement—one that brings the mosaic of ethnicity to this world, symbolizing the one to come. Such unity is not uniformity—it must define the Church as it faces all the political, economic, and philosophical ideas which are warring to divide it. Until Christians are troubled and discontent that the gospel of consumerism is more diverse and uniting than the Gospel of salvation, churches should expect to see a curious world skip by these homogeneous enclaves and forage for meaningful connection wherever it can be found.

Multiculturalism is important to any church leader desiring to reach his or her world today. Every day, newscasts carry the story of tension in race relations. Sunday remains the most segregated hour of the week. What is the local church to do? No matter where you are, God can use you to help heal this continent's racial divisions and make Sunday morning look a lot more like heaven. Ed Stetzer, in his *Christianity Today* article titled, "Challenges to Becoming a Multicultural Church," lists four strategic principles for a local church to become more multicultural—no matter where the church is located:

(1) *Notice the neighborhood.* Is your neighborhood

changing? There is one Pentecostal church in a major city that moves every time the ethnic makeup of their neighborhood changes. Don't move out; move in!

(2) *Become a welcoming and understanding community.* Many times, we don't know how an ethnically diverse person feels, because we are of a different ethnic culture. Hispanics do not truly know how it feels to be black. An African American does not know how it feels to be Asian. However, we do know how it feels to be human, no matter who we are.

(3) *Hire leadership that represents your values.* Where possible, make sure different ethnicities are well represented on church boards, deacon committees, volunteer ministries, and church marketing.

(4) *Always focus on the big picture.* What is the big picture? Ed Stetzer reminds us that it's the reconciliation of the human race to God!

In an article on "Seven Steps to Becoming a Multiethnic Church," Aubrey Malphurs gives one final admonition to leading the church to renew its

Reaching Wherever You Are

commitment to ethnic inclusion: "It must be intentional!" It isn't going to happen by accident.

3. Marketplace Incarnation Can Happen, No Matter Where You Are

The Gospel message started with an incarnation, and it can spread only through contextual incarnation. In other words, the message of Christ must be taken and communicated in the language of the people we are trying to reach. Different places will require different strategies, using the same absolute truths found in the Scriptures. For example, Acts 17:17 says, "Therefore he reasoned in the synagogue with the Jews and with the Gentile worshipers, and in the marketplace daily with those who happened to be there" (NKJV).

The city of Athens in the first century is surprisingly like many American cities of the 21st century. Urban communities today have poverty, but they are not impoverished. They have wealth, but they are not rich. American cities are highly educated, yet they are filled with underperforming schools. There is violence and crime, yet celebrations of life and the arts exist. Cities tend to be philosophically and politically progressive, yet they are deeply proud of their unique history and cultural

AWAKENING THE CHURCH IN NORTH AMERICA

status. Possibly the most significant similarity between the ancient Athenians and our modern urban dwellers is that both are quite religious and, paradoxically, extremely secular; so much so, secularism itself often becomes the religion of choice for the urban professional. It was to this environment the apostle Paul was called; it is to this urban humanity that the Church must answer its calling. The church, according to pastor Tobey Montgomery (Oakland, California), must present the Gospel in three ways—incarnationally, relationally, and transformationally.

• *The Gospel of Jesus is incarnational.* The sovereign hand of Almighty God has ordered our steps, our times, and our places (see Acts 17:26). An older servant of God once testified that when he "received the Holy Ghost, he got the holy *go!*" Many love the concept of souls being saved, but they do not want to be around lost people. Church members want a revival in the cities, lamenting their decay, but they will not go there! Paul went to Athens, to the synagogue, and into the marketplace. The Lord calls His disciples to go and actively engage within the cultural arena (see Luke 19:10).

• *The Gospel is relational.* Jesus did not arrive on earth on a

REACHING WHEREVER YOU ARE

Thursday, die on Friday, resurrect on Sunday, and leave on Monday. He came to live and build relationships, making a way for humankind to become the children of God. Therefore, His ministry is the believer's ministry, and it is relational—reaching, embracing, and bearing the woundedness of souls for His sake.

In Athens, Paul first reached out to the Diaspora within the synagogue community. He reasoned with those of similar beliefs, values, and backgrounds. This is a sound practice, provided Christians do not limit the ministry to their own regional, cultural, or ethnic "diaspora." Followers of Christ must have an effective ministry within the "synagogue" *and* in the "marketplace." In Oakland, we seek to build relational bridges through the arts, education, practical support, and proclaiming the good news in a manner the community understands. While never compromising the Gospel, we desire to value the divine dignity and eternal worth of every soul within our city (see Romans 1:14; 1 Corinthians 9:19-23).

• *The Gospel is transformational.* Like Paul in Athens, churches must reach and relate, but with humility, acknowledging that intelligence, communication skills, and courage are no substitute for the supernatural power of God! The

Gospel is not merely persuading the mind, clothing the body, or feeding the stomach; it is also the transforming power of Jesus Christ (Romans 1:16; 1 Corinthians 2:1-5). Only Jesus can save a soul, change a nation, or set the captives free. As Paul demonstrated in Athens—there is no other remedy (see Acts 17:30-31).

4. God Can Give You Divine Revelation, No Matter Where You Are

Whatever the location, the guidance of the Holy Spirit is needed for success. The Holy Spirit can guide churches and individuals toward transformation and revitalization. The Holy Spirit is a wise leader who knows how to renew every aspect of life. The Holy Spirit can speak to those who are listening and bring fresh revelation and knowledge!

Doyle Roberts believes divine revelation is key, no matter the setting or location. Matthew 16:13-19 reveals the importance of revelation. In the last portion of verse 18, Jesus says, "On this rock I will build My church, and the gates of Hades shall not prevail against it" (NKJV).

This scripture is two-edged. The first revelation is that Jesus is the Rock. Second, He wants to reveal His specific plan for our lives. When someone receives that

REACHING WHEREVER YOU ARE

revelation, the gates of hell will not prevail against the plan He has for their lives. There will be times in ministry, that had it not been for the vision (the previous revelation God provided) a pastor or church might not have survived the attacks of the Enemy. Revelation is a key in building the Church.

Pastor John Ulrich asks a powerful question that relates to Roberts' experience of building a healthy, strong church in Columbia, South Carolina. He asks, "How do you know where to go and what to do?" When building the house of God, knowing what to do is not always clear! Pastor Ulrich suggests remembering three significant promises found in Acts 1:1-11. Jesus assures:

- *Power*: to enable, authorize, and strengthen
- *Purpose*: The Great Commission is the assigned objective.
- *Presence*: The Holy Spirit is a gift to every leader. The Holy Spirit is the best GPS a leader could ever dream of having as he or she builds a church.

Divine revelation is fundamental to ministry success.

5. God Wants You to Establish Justice, No Matter Where You Are

The Bible says, "Justice, and only justice, you shall

pursue" (Deuteronomy 16:20 NASB). Most Christians think very little about their role in speaking up for the those who have no voice. They do so without ever noticing the message behind the exodus of Moses. Speaking up for the poor, the voiceless, the disenfranchised, and the forgotten were the leadership characteristics that defined Moses. Many people are burdened by the power of others and troubled because of their economic status in society, which may cause the masses to overlook their importance. It is easy to look past the sightless, ignore the voiceless, or oppress the resourceless. However, God's people should speak for those with no vision, voice, or resources. The Scriptures teaches: "This is what is required of you, that you do justice, love kindness, and walk humbly before the Lord your God" (Micah 6:8, paraphrase).

Pastor Bruce Deel found himself living in a sixty-five-year-old church building in the inner city of Atlanta with his wife and five daughters. This scenario was not on his ministerial bucket list. Some disciples are called to undesirable and even dangerous places. When someone launches a benevolent, nonprofit church where regular break-ins occur and protecting important items from being stolen is required, it can seem rather stressful

REACHING WHEREVER YOU ARE

compared to doing ministry in the suburbs. However, God calls and leads believers to be champions of justice.

What is meant by the phrase, "Do justice"? It can mean feeding the hungry; housing the homeless poor; rescuing those being trafficked and abused sexually; creating employment opportunities for citizens returning from incarceration and drug-and-alcohol treatment facilities; building a clinic to provide medical, dental, vision, and mental-health care. It may mean building a private daycare and Christian school, serving children and teens from poverty environments, or speaking up for those without a voice. Biblically, these actions set a church in the right direction for doing justice.

Like Bruce Deel, God can use others who are willing to administer justice, no matter where they are. For this inner-city Atlanta ministry some twenty-one years later, *justice* is a 210,000-square-foot building in Georgia's most challenged neighborhood with twelve satellite locations around the country. Justice is the construction of a forty-seven-unit apartment community to serve individuals who have survived without support systems, yet they wish to thrive. Justice is represented in the long, slow walk with more than 20,000 souls who have benefitted from the

AWAKENING THE CHURCH IN NORTH AMERICA

services offered by City of Refuge—a place where light, hope, and transformation are shared daily.

When considering the plight of his hometown, Nehemiah was asked by the king, "What would you have me do?" (2:4, paraphrase). Nehemiah responded, "If it please the king . . . send me" (v. 5 KJV). *Doing justice* means that followers of Christ reply the same way: "Send me." Perhaps God has placed you where justice is needed—where your voice is needed to speak for those who cannot speak for themselves. No matter the location, there is always someone who needs a Christian to speak up for them.

In his book, *Generous Justice*, Tim Keller says justice has four qualities:

(1) *Justice cares for the vulnerable.* In Lesotho, South Africa, one pastor found himself wrestling with the call to speak up for those with no voice. This pastor discovered a twelve-year-old girl living in a house by herself. Her parents had died of AIDS. She was vulnerable, scared, and being intimidated by an uncle who had tried to rape her and then take her home. The pastor thought to himself, *I will call the. . . .* At that moment, he realized there were no police on this off-beaten path in a

REACHING WHEREVER YOU ARE

country with the fifth-highest poverty rate in the world. There was no available justice to protect, speak for, or keep this vulnerable orphan girl safe. The only voice she had that day was a pastor who made the decision to speak up for her. God's call is to care for the defenseless and unprotected.

(2) *Justice reflects on the character of God.* God speaks for the poor, and He expects His people to do so as well. Proverbs 29:7 reflects such qualities.

(3) *Justice focuses on right relationships.* In Cleveland, Tennessee, there is a new program called City Fields, and it is working in conjunction with the Police Department, the United Way, the Cleveland City Mayor's Office, and other agencies. The strategy is enormously productive; it is changing a specific impoverished community in Bradley County. How do they shut down meth houses, pave sidewalks, plant trees, help the poor own their own homes, build new parks, and more? It is all done through relationships.

(4) *Justice includes generosity.* Regardless of locale, generosity can change a city. In 2 Timothy, we are provided with several principles to prepare God's

people for the second coming of Jesus Christ. It describes the kind of world that will exist when this time reveals itself. One of the defining characteristics will be the essential absence of love and kindness toward other humans. God can use the kindness of His children to change a city. Generosity breaks down the hardest of hearts, no matter the environment.

6. Love Can Make a Difference, No Matter Where You Are

Justice is a great lead-in for this fundamental principle of "no matter where you are." People who go through painful moments in life have often successfully disconnected from much of the world. They appear hard, unreachable, and often hostile. First John 4:8 says, "God is love" (KJV). His love really can surmount the most improbable height, scale the longest offense, and successfully ascend the peak of the tallest hostilities. Love makes a difference in anyone, no matter who or where they are.

Teams from Men and Women of Action (MWOA), an outreach ministry of the Church of God, have learned that no matter the geographic or social position, love

REACHING WHEREVER YOU ARE

works. Bob Pace, MWOA founder, shared his dream of demonstrating the love of Christ in practical ways with a few close friends. Since 1983, MWOA has completed almost 2,500 meaningful projects in more than 80 countries and in all 50 states. More than 5,600 men and women have volunteered their time, skills, and money to participate in these building, repair, and restoration projects.

Teddie Bennett, a member of MWOA, often points others to Matthew 25:40, which says, "Inasmuch as you did it to one of the least of these My brethren, you did it to Me" (NKJV). God wants pastors, leaders, and laity to show people God's heart through love in action to whomever. Born-again believers must be love in action. John 13:35 unmistakably conveys that nothing demonstrates the character of a true disciple more than love when Jesus said, "By this all will know that you are My disciples, if you have love one for another" (NKJV).

7. God Knows Exactly How to Renew Everything, No Matter Where You Are

Discouragement is almost automatic when the road ahead looks hard, long, and difficult. But followers of Jesus find encouragement knowing God placed them

AWAKENING THE CHURCH IN NORTH AMERICA

exactly where He intended. The Lord can use anyone who is willing to allow Him to do so, within any setting. Christians and ministry leaders often need renewal to recognize the opportunity for a spiritual awakening in their city, town, or community. It is possible! In fact, God has placed a seed of renewal in every living thing He has made, including every pastor and every church member. All living things have seeds deep within—the power to renew and reproduce. So it is with the Gospel in your city, town, or region.

To those needing God to renew, remember this: It is natural for life to reproduce itself, to divide, to die, and to re-create. It is perfectly normal for the living Church to renew itself. In 1734, God used Jonathan Edwards; in the 1700's, He used George Whitefield, who spoke to 80 percent of the 900,000 American colonists. In the 1800's, when only one in fifteen Americans attended an Evangelical church, He used James McGready at Cane Ridge. In the same century, God used Charles Finney to lead more than 500,000 people to Christ. He also used D. L. Moody to speak to more than 2,500,000 people. In 1906, the Lord used William J. Seymour at Azusa Street to ignite a Pentecostal revival. Today, He wants to use

180

REACHING WHEREVER YOU ARE

you, no matter where you are. Living things were created to renew themselves naturally. Hold on. Don't give up. Renewal is coming!

Max DePree describes an important principle about the courage to lead renewal. "In the end, it is important to remember that we cannot become what we need to be by remaining what we are." Also, William G. McLoughlin, a leader in awakenings, revivals, and reforms proposed that renewal is not just about the local church, but rather the entire community. "Revivals alter the lives of individuals; awakenings alter the worldview of a whole people or culture."

8. A Soul Matters, No Matter Where You Are

There are many times when a passionate believer in Christ feels the need to pack up and move to a foreign land to work for God. However, no matter the location, God wants to use everyone to win souls. Jesus said, "You will receive power when the Holy Spirit comes on you; and you will be my witnesses in Jerusalem, and in all Judea and Samaria, and to the ends of the earth" (Acts 1:8 NIV).

Lost people don't just show up at church anymore, and this is a game-changer. Jesus said, "Go!" He did

AWAKENING THE CHURCH IN NORTH AMERICA

not say to wait for them to come to the church. To get average Christian people to "go," they must be recruited, equipped, and held accountable.

Richard Dial planted a church in Ecuador and realized the impact there could also be realized here in America, so he planted thirteen churches. At one of them, the church-plant leaders prayed with more than seven hundred adults to accept Christ as their Lord and Savior!

The same principles used abroad can also be used to take a "short-term mission trip at home" here in North America. Here is how:

(1) Cover everything with organized prayer.

(2) Challenge people in a Sunday-morning church service to join the mission team that is going to share the Gospel with the people within their town and circle of influence.

(3) Team members must commit to sharing the Gospel with at least one person during the mission month.

(4) Gather the team once a week, for one month, for prayer and preparation.

(5) The training should primarily be coaching, not lecture style.

REACHING WHEREVER YOU ARE

(6) Conduct a "sending service" for the mission team in a Sunday service. Invite the congregation to pray with them.

(7) Place each member of the mission team on a "Go Action Team" consisting of no more than five individuals. The team's purpose is to pray together, encourage each other, coach each other, and hold each another accountable.

(8) The team meets as the month begins and after each week ends.

(9) The "home missionaries" should ask the Lord, "Who do You want me to share Christ with?"

(10) Once identified, they should cultivate a friendship. The unsaved person needs to know they are cared for.

(11) Missionaries extend an invitation to their friend to meet and get better acquainted.

(12) The missionary should begin the conversation by asking questions about their friend's life history.

(13) Eventually, an opportunity will come for the missionary to share about himself or herself and his or her testimony.

(14) This testimony should consist of what life was

like before he or she came to Jesus, how he or she came to Jesus, and what life is like now.

(15) Then, the missionary should ask the question: "If you were to stand before God today and He were to ask you, 'Why should I let you in to My heaven?' what would you say?"

(16) The missionary should allow them to answer and then assure them that God wants them in His heaven.

(17) The missionary should then share the Gospel with the friend. (A Gospel app previously loaded on the missionary's phone might be used.)

(18) Next, the home missionary asks their friend if they want to accept the gift of eternal life. If the answer is yes, lead them in a prayer of repentance and acceptance of God's grace.

(19) Finally, they should invite their friend to get together again and talk about how to follow Jesus.

It is not required to go to a foreign country, as great as that is, to be used by God. North America needs Christian people to focus on her, too! In the USA, one out of three adults (33%) are unchurched. This number represents nearly 125 million people, which if that were a country,

REACHING WHEREVER YOU ARE

would make it the tenth-largest country in the world. Jeff Schapiro of the *Christian Post* calls the United States the "fastest-growing mission field in the world." While some erroneously assume the USA is "over-churched," the truth is, Americans are dramatically unchurched. Dave Olson indicates that, in America, there were:

- Twenty-eight churches for every 10,000 people in 1900.
- Seventeen churches for every 10,000 people in 1950.
- Twelve churches for every 10,000 people in 2000.
- Eleven churches for every 10,000 people in 2010.

The difficult, yet still exciting, truth is this: Weekly church attendance in America plummeted from an average of 20.4 percent weekly in 1990, to 17.5 percent weekly in 2005. How is that "good news?" The harvest is plentiful. There are more people not going to church in each city than there are available seats in the churches. Think about that. Every believer has the possibility to fill their church sanctuary this Sunday—no matter where that church is located!

9. Never Say, "It's Just Bethlehem," No Matter Where You Are

Sometimes people can feel as if their small town or rural area is not as important in the eyes of God as cities like New York or Los Angeles. There are times when God will speak to people with the capability to pastor in a mega-city, but God's will is for them to plant a mega-vision in a smaller place. Some pastors may feel like Jonah being told to go to Nineveh. They might think, *God, You have the wrong number!* Some might ask: *How can I dream in that town? How will I reach the world from this little place?* No matter where one finds himself or herself, don't limit the vision to the size of a town—only by the size of God. The following list provides some things every Christian from a smaller town or community needs to know about dreaming in Bethlehem:

Great things can come out of Bethlehem; things that can change the world. Never limit the vision by eyesight, the economy, or the obvious traditions there.

• Never let a boot tell a foot how big it is going to get. A dreamer can excel and reach the masses in a small town.

• Pastoring a successful church in a small community doesn't mean someone is less capable than those pastoring in a large city. Those who have done so will

REACHING WHEREVER YOU ARE

say it takes more leadership, excellence, commitment, and strategy to succeed in a small town than it does in a larger community. A small-town pastor must go on all six cylinders consistently!

• God can send competent people in a small town to help. Growth is often challenging in a smaller community because it is not always the most popular place to serve. God knows how to send capable team members to assist. Past relationships are invaluable as a ministry team comes together. The common denominator of building a great team in a small town is capitalizing on three key things—relationships, relationships, and relationships.

• God can provide resources in small towns. Remember, money follows anointed, productive, significant ministry. No matter the location or size of the town, pastors and leaders must dream, succeed, and push the envelope for the glory of God, reawakening North America.

10. Babylon Can Be Won, No Matter Where You Are

It may be tempting to give up when praying for a city like Chicago or Toronto to "wake up." However, an awakening is possible in North America's largest cities. Cities with a vast population are central to the heart of

AWAKENING THE CHURCH IN NORTH AMERICA

God. Jesus always made the salvation of souls His priority. Cities shape nations; therefore, reaching cities must be a priority. According to *U.S.A. Today*, all but one of the United States' largest cities are experiencing population growth. In the USA, there are about 330 million people; 25 million of those people live in the top ten largest cities. When the suburbs are added to these numbers, nearly one half of America lives in largely populated territories. According to the U.S. Census Bureau, large American cities are home to 62.7 percent of the population. Remarkably, these cities represent a population density of 46 times more than that of territories outside the cities. This represents an average of 1,593 people per square mile! Obviously, cities are so important to the mission of God.

Hugh Nelson went to New York City to pastor a great church. He says one of the most important objectives in reaching a city is to focus on wining souls. Jesus said, "Occupy till I come" (Luke 19:13 KJV). He said these words as He gave the parable of the pounds in Luke 19, and it took place in the large city of Jericho. Jesus had just encountered Zacchaeus, the chief publican of Jericho, and witnessed his subsequent transformation. Zacchaeus

Reaching Wherever You Are

was a wealthy tax collector earning his income primarily by deceit and theft. Although dishonest and despised by the people, Zacchaeus' desire to see Jesus stirred him to run ahead of the crowd and position himself in a tree to see the approaching Messiah. When Jesus drew near, He looked up and instructed Zacchaeus to come down quickly, because Jesus desired to visit his home. Zacchaeus hastily descended and joyfully led Jesus to his home.

This gesture of compassion from Jesus toward a sinner caused the crowd to question and murmur. In his quest to demonstrate a changed life, Zacchaeus declared his intent to donate half of his possessions to the poor and give a fourfold restoration to anyone he had cheated. Jesus, in response, declared that this day salvation came to the house of Zacchaeus and affirmed that the former corrupt official was also a son of Abraham.

The parable that follows indicates the people were caught up in the wave of Messianic expectations and lacked appreciation for the conversion taking place right in front of them. This sudden expectation of the Kingdom and dreams of freedom from Roman oppression made them oblivious to their earthly redemptive responsibilities. So many Christians today, in preparation for Christ's return,

Awakening the Church in North America

are withdrawing from engaging with secular with society while forgetting that many like Zacchaeus still desire an encounter with God. Jesus went home with the most despised person in Jericho that day because His mission of salvation remained His priority.

This story confirms that when just one soul is won in a large city, it can become a catalyst for tremendous change. Therefore, cities play an enormous part in bringing change to culture. Cities are full of people who influence and inform culture. Whereas, in a small area, one may reach a few lawyers or a few physicians, in a large city, pastors and church members may influence the people who train lawyers and physicians by speaking to the guilds that organize those institutions. Cities are where culture is created, and a church that reaches the city is a church that influences the culture.

Also, cities play a pivotal role in shaping the culture of nations. It is a place to engage even the most despised. Pastor Nelson went to New York. New York City has a population of more than 9 million people with eight hundred languages spoken there, which provides a rich opportunity to reach people regardless of their status in life.

Babylon may look intimidating; it may seem like an impossible place for God to awaken. However, God can reach any modern-day Babylon, no matter where it is.

Right Where You Are

These ten strategies clearly show how hope can become a reality, no matter where someone is serving God. God is not a respecter of persons. He knows no difficulty between reaching Babylon or birthing something great out of Bethlehem.

> **These ten strategies clearly show how hope can become a reality, no matter where someone is serving God.**

He travels the boroughs of New York City as easily as He does the small place of Lambert Town, South Carolina. No street can hide from His influence, and no rolling hill on the American countryside can escape the power of His vision. God has the knowledge and power to contextualize the Gospel in any city's culture, no matter where you are!

AWAKENING THE CHURCH IN NORTH AMERICA

Collaborative Team Members for "Reaching Wherever You Are"

Michael Knight, Collaborative Coach
Lead Pastor, Life Builders Church of God,
Madisonville, Kentucky

Teddie Bennett
Administrative Director, Men and Women of Action,
Church of God, Cleveland, Tennessee

Bryan Cutshall
President, Church Trainer, Cleveland, Tennessee

Bruce Deel
CEO, City of Refuge, Midtown, Atlanta, Georgia

Richard Dial
Bishop, Missionary Church Planter,
Morrisville, North Carolina

Kyle Hinson
Lead Pastor, Spring Valley Church of God,
Reading, Pennsylvania

Tobey Montgomery
Pastor, Christian Cathedral, Oakland, California

R. C. Hugh Nelson
Senior Pastor, Church of God East Flatbush,
Brooklyn, New York

REACHING WHEREVER YOU ARE

B. Doyle Roberts
Lead Pastor, International Praise Church of God,
Columbia, South Carolina

8

AWAKEN TO YOUR PURPOSE!

"To everything there is a season, a time for every purpose under heaven" (Ecclesiastes 3:1 NKJV).

Waking up each day is usually pleasant for me. It begins in my mind before my eyes are open. I realize my thoughts are flowing and I am thinking about something to do in my new day. I open my eyes, stretch, place my feet on the floor, and stand.

However, there have been days when I experienced a rude awakening. I hate rude awakenings—they are surprising, unpleasant discoveries, bothering me with something unwanted or unneeded.

In the natural world and in life, seasons come that offer windows of opportunity. Recognizing the seasons and finding the courage to respond is the key to your purpose and life's meaning. Imagine realizing, too late, that you had been on the threshold of greatness but missed the opportunity. To avoid this kind of rude awakening, you must be aware of your purpose, be bathed in prayer, and follow awareness with decisive action.

No one person in the church will likely make a difference by trying to change the minds or actions of others, but he or she can personally model the change that is needed to influence others. As a leader, you may be the only one who understands what should change. The changes may feel odd, and perhaps seem counterproductive. But, with humility and love for all, your mission is to pursue the God-given opportunity with all your heart.

A partnership between pastors and leaders can navigate the sometimes-painful journey of change. Inevitably, change challenges the process that has traditionally been embraced. This is uncomfortable to the people who have been in church for years. Remember, they are products of their environment, believing and doing what they were told by their former leaders. They did not become what they are today all by themselves. Every one of them deserves the longsuffering and grace God has given you.

Leaders must be sure that the present members believe they are just as valuable and important as new people. Healthy change employs the spirit of *reconstruction*, not *deconstruction*.

Honoring Legacy Leads to Healthy Change

A good practice when working toward change is for pastors to remind people of their heritage; ring the legacy bell. Speak about the *who, what, why,* and *how* of the history and mission of your church. Reminding them of the church's purpose from its beginning requires constant communication and is spiritually fundamental for an awakening or turnaround.

Pastors should get the influencers in the church involved in prayer and conversation. Discuss possibilities of reaching out to unsaved and unchurched people. Be quick to show and promise respect to the veteran members—the people who have served Christ and sacrificed to support His church. When pastors aren't able to achieve consensus, they should back up for a couple of weeks, and then bring back the idea again and ask if they will support a reasonable effort. People are honored when their concerns are listened to and when they are asked for their blessing.

Many years ago, I came across research indicating that, over time, organizations become more distant between

AWAKENING THE CHURCH IN NORTH AMERICA

the head and the corpus. Even with this awareness, it still happens—institutions unwittingly adapt to policies that sustain the office instead of serving people.

It is human to need a reminder of our purpose and what is supposed to be happening in the Church. Jesus promised in John 7:38, "He who believes in Me, as the Scripture has said, out of his heart will flow rivers of living water" (NKJV).

Where's the water now? Too many of us have received living water but have hoarded it in private reservoirs. Too many churches have become "Dead Seas" that do not produce life. We are to be wells, not cisterns—bubbling with fresh water instead of just storing it for some "future" use. Unlike a cemetery that buries the community, the Church is to bring life to the community.

"We Do Not Have Enough . . . "
—Wrong Answer!

This tendency to become an inactive Christian is to become defeated—heavy-laden with doubt and unbelief. However, to hide quietly, abiding in a *"que sera, sera"* code of conduct is essentially sinful. Today's average congregation is like the disciples who were convinced every good thing God was going to do had already been done. Church members look at their situation and, just like the disciples before Jesus fed the 5,000, say: "This is a desert place, and the time is now past" (Matthew 14:15 KJV). They go about their lives with the mentality that nothing can be done. With God's help, the Church must lose the "we-don't-have-enough" attitude Andrew blindly claimed in John 6:9 when he asked, "But what are they [five loaves and two fishes] among so many?"

Even in desert places and in the "what-I-do-doesn't-matter" assessment of the situation, Jesus always has a plan! His plan is of His own will and doesn't show up on most people's radar. Because Christians do not know and cannot see what He sees, they must act in faith, instead of by sight or feelings.

Wake Up and Go!

Visiting hundreds of churches for more than four decades has revealed one of the church's greatest sins. For clarity, I speak of sin from an understanding of sin as a failure, being in error, missing the mark (ἁμαρτία, *hamartia*). The sin referred to here is easily overlooked and often excused. It is a tragic sin, like that of the steward who buried his talent instead of risking it to gain an increase. Much of the Church holds to a belief that what

AWAKENING THE CHURCH IN NORTH AMERICA

they say or do doesn't make a difference—so it becomes easy to do nothing at all. There are many people sitting in the pews of churches who believe they have nothing to contribute. They feel as if their contributions carry no weight, or they have no influence. What is this great sin that affects so many? *The sin is underestimating what an individual and local church can do for God's glory.* This is both sad and wrong.

> **Much of the Church holds to a belief that what they say or do doesn't make a difference—so it becomes easy to do nothing at all.**

I love to remind people that they are important to the Kingdom and they can make a difference. While Paul insists not to "think more highly [of ourselves] than [we] ought," he also says to think soberly, knowing that all Christians are given a "measure of faith" (see Romans 12:3). This gift of faith enables each disciple of Jesus to be useful in the body of Christ. As Paul points out in his letters, especially in Romans 12; 2 Corinthians 12–14; and Ephesians 4, it is time for every Christian to take on apostolic confidence as expressed in Philippians 4:13 when he announced, "I can do all things through Christ who strengthens me" (NKJV).

Believers must adopt the individual motto of the "ten most powerful two-letter words" in the English language: "If it is to be, it is up to me!"

The preaching of the Word must target not only preparing the saints for heaven, but also for unifying them on earth and sending them to active duty in the harvest. As mentioned previously, Barna research suggests 57 percent of Christian Millennials believe it is wrong to *evangelize*—to attempt to convert nonbelievers to Christ. Similarly, Fuller Institute research projects that 87 percent of current church members do not know what "body part" they are in the body of Christ. Christians need purpose, direction, and passion.

Spiritual renewal is more than church growth or a surface change in structure. The Church must consistently reform its culture to have the Romans 8:31 enthusiasm that infused the early Church in Acts, as well as early Pentecostalism a hundred years ago. An authentic awakening is not more self-confidence, but rather more Holy Spirit-dependence. As believers truly grasp that the Holy Spirit is our Helper who guides, teaches, and clothes with supernatural power, hope, passion, and zeal are restored. In this season, allow the Holy Spirit to awaken you, awaken your church and awaken the Church in North America.

Endorsements

What resonates is the writer's desire to convey the importance of Christ's Church and how we can ensure her success. . . . The Church holds the answer for what ails North America.

Yvette Santana
Director, Women's Discipleship Ministries
Southwest Hispanic Region
Upland, California

Awakening the Church in North America, reminds me of the importance and value of staying focused on our task to win souls for the Kingdom.

Keith L. Ivester
National Bishop
Canada

If you care about the Church in North America, and more importantly, its vital mission, then you will benefit greatly from the poignant and insightful wisdom (and answers) found in these pages.

David L. Kemp
Administrative Bishop
North Central Region
Bismarck, North Dakota

AWAKENING THE CHURCH IN NORTH AMERICA

This book encourages the Church to awaken from its slumber and recapture her true calling. Bishop Stephens reveals the needed changes in the church and provides solutions for the future.

Emma Byrd
Lee University freshman
Cleveland, Tennessee

Jim Stephens has served the Church of God in the highest leadership positions in this continent's two largest countries. His personal life and professional experience speak volumes.

Marc-Elie Morisset
Pastor, Outremont and Rock of Ages Churches of God
Montreal and Ottawa, Canada

This book is filled with Scripture and stories that point to healthy Church. All of them contribute to fulfilling this statement: "It is time to reclaim the Church and its importance in the kingdom of God."

Jerald Daffe, D.Min.
Professor of Pastoral Studies
Lee University
Cleveland, Tennessee

I highly recommend this valuable tool to all who sense the rising tide of last-day urgency and want to be part of the harvest.

Toby Morgan
Administrative Bishop
Weatherford, Texas